eat! enjoy!

THE LIFETRACK COOKBOOK

Many thanks to the entire team at the Australian Cancer Society's Lifetrack Program; especially Ray Baxter, Paul Davey and Maree Davidson; and to the participants in the program for the support and information required to produce this book. To the celebrity food lovers who enthusiastically gave of their time, expertise and recipes. To Sally Kaptein, Tony Khan and Janet Lillie who produced and tested many of the recipes. To the production team who have brought the information to life for us all to enjoy, namely Saskia Ericson, whose design and illustrations reflect the vitality of eating for fun and fervour; James Vlahogiannis and Janet Lillie whose stunning photography and food styling carry the message further; Julie Woods for her 'food not nutrients' focus and attention to detail and Foong Ling Kong for her encouragement and editing.

A special thanks to Gordon and Barry Hill at Hillman Cycles in West Brunswick, for providing the bicycle pictured on page 142. Thanks also to Birds Eye Edgell and Kelloggs for their support of the Lifetrack Program and for providing ingredients used in recipe-testing.

THE LIFETRACK COOKBOOK

Vikki Leng

with contributions from

Allan Campion, Michele Curtis, Duré-Dara, Gabriel Gaté,

Athol Guy, Karen Inge, Geoff Jansz, Sally Kaptein, Tony Khan,

Janet Lillie, Ian Parmenter, Catherine Saxelby,

Rosemary Stanton, Lyn Talbot and Julie Woods.

Lifetrack

National Library of Australia
Cataloguing-in-Publication data:
Leng, Vikki, 1951–
    Eat! Enjoy!: the Lifetrack cookbook.

    Includes index.
    ISBN 0 947283 63 3.

    1. High-fiber diet–Recipes. 2. Low-fat diet–Recipes.
    3. Cookery (Natural Foods).
    I. Anti-Cancer Council of Victoria. II. Title.

641.302

Photography by James Vlahogiannis
Food styling by Janet Lillie
Food styling assistance by Tiffany Page
Art direction by Saskia Ericson and Vikki Leng
Design and illustrations by Saskia Ericson
Printed by Bambra Press

Front Cover: Chilli Avocado Steaks with Onion & Tomato Salsa (page 112)
Back Cover: Roasted Pumpkin & Beetroot Salad (page 44)

FoReWoRD

There is now overwhelming evidence that what we eat and how it is prepared plays a vital role in determining our health and wellbeing.

It is equally clear that in addition to the right food, enjoyment and ease of preparation are key ingredients if our aim is to establish and maintain a healthy and well-balanced diet. *Eat! Enjoy!* is just the cookbook to show us how to do it.

Based on the recommendations of the successful Lifetrack Dietary Assessment Program, popular food and nutrition author Vikki Leng and her team have created an exciting array of simple-to-prepare recipes that are not only nutritious and delicious, but take into account our busy lifestyles. So if you want nutritious food that is fast, fun and full of flavour, then this is the cookbook for you. Eat! Enjoy!

Professor Robert Burton
Director
Anti-Cancer Council of Victoria

Contents

INtRoDuctioN

Eat! Enjoy! is packed with exciting recipes that spell out health and happiness. They are light, healthy, bursting with colour and flavour, and as if that isn't enough, they are quick and easy to prepare.

Eat! Enjoy! has been written for everyone who loves good food including those who enjoy healthy eating. Following the overwhelming public response to the Australian Cancer Society's Lifetrack program, a cry for 'more recipes!' was heard far and wide. (To find out all about the innovative Lifetrack program, turn to Chapter 7 'Get Your Life on Track with Lifetrack'.)

Eat! Enjoy! embraces true enjoyment of food and life – even shopping and cooking. Flip though the book and you'll find many recipes that are sure to tempt your taste buds. The colour pics really tell the story, so you won't even have to read a word to understand the excitement of preparing light, bright, easy-to-cook, easy-to-eat dishes.

Celebrity food lovers from around Australia, including Allan Campion, Michele Curtis, Duré-Dara, Gabriel Gaté, Karen Inge, Geoff Jansz, Ian Parmenter, Catherine Saxelby and Rosemary Stanton, many of whom provided recipes for inclusion in the *Lifetrack 2000 Dietary Guide,* have continued their enthusiastic support by contributing some exciting new recipes to this book.

Passionate food lovers Sally Kaptein, Janet Lillie, Tony Khan and dietitian Julie Woods helped me come up with a diverse range of recipes that not only tantalise the senses, but have been nutritionally analysed to ensure they meet current dietary recommendations.

Looking for an exciting way to serve bananas? Try *Banana Brûlée with Citrus Salsa*. Thought sandwiches were boring? Try *Vegie Wraps* and *Chicken, Tabouli & Nori Wraps*. Is your life lacking colour and vitality? Go for *Psychedelic Sauce with Creamy Polenta*. For a sweet touch, it's hard to go past *Mini Mango Freezecakes*. And when the going gets tough, try getting tender with comfort foods such as *Ian Parmenter's Lamb Shank & Tomato Ragout* or *Honest to Goodness Beef Stew*. And if you can't stand the heat in the kitchen, take a break, and cool down with icy-cold *Cherry Freezes*, or sit back and relax with *Vanilla Iced Coffee on the Rocks*.

To make it easier to create delicious dishes according to what you have on hand, and to help you find recipes which are based on foods that you want to eat more of, *Eat! Enjoy!* is divided into chapters according to particular foods. Chapter 6 'Fast Foods at Home' will get you out of trouble if you haven't shopped for some time yet don't want to rely on take-away fast foods. The key to getting fast at home is to have a well-stocked pantry and freezer, so we have included a *Freezer & Pantry Checklist* to get you started. Then you will be able to treat yourself to delicious and nutritious dishes such as: *Spinach Enchiladas; Pepper Crusted Rack of Lamb with Plum & Cranberry Sauce;* and *Jambalaya*, a New Orleans version of the renowned Spanish paella.

More good news! The Lifetrack program considers the social aspects of enjoying food and accepts the inclusion of less healthy food choices – in small amounts or occasionally. We have consequently included some notes with several recipes, such as *Maple Berry Sauce*, 'Pour this beautiful sauce onto serving plates, top with slices of your favourite chocolate cake and serve scattered with even more berries' – on occasion of course! So, from all of us, what more can we say but – eat, enjoy!

Vikki Leng, on behalf of the team

This page: *Vegie Wraps* (page 25)
Opposite: *Rice Volcano* (page 24) with *Roasted Red Capsicum Sauce* (page 35)

eat! enjoy!

Breads & Cereals

Breads, cereals and cereal products, including muesli, oats, couscous, pasta and rice are high-carbohydrate, high-performance foods. Here you'll find a range of delicious dishes to help you kickstart your day and keep you going well into the night!

Karen Inge's
Bircher Muesli

Karen Inge is a dietitian who specialises in sports nutrition. She is Director of the Institute of Health and Fitness in Melbourne and Sports Nutrition Coordinator for the Victorian Institute of Sport. Karen is vice-president of Sports Dietitians Australia, and is an ambassador for VicHealth. She is the nutrition writer for the Australian Womens Weekly and has her own column 'Food for Thought' in The Age. Karen has also written several books: the latest is *Food for Sport Cookbook*.

According to Karen, 'Consuming carbohydrate-rich foods regularly throughout the day helps maximise our energy levels, fuel our fitness and boost our vitality.' A great place to start is at the beginning, with breakfast! Enjoy this low-fat version of ever popular Bircher Muesli which is laden with carbohydrate and plenty of other goodies such as vitamins, minerals and dietary fibre.

2 cups rolled oats

²/₃ cup orange juice

1 cup apricot-flavoured Jalna BioGarde Drinking Yoghurt

1 cup plain skim-milk yoghurt

2 tablespoons honey

1 cup sultanas

1 cup sliced fruit such as bananas, apple and strawberries

¹/₂ cup slivered almonds

1. Combine the oats, orange juice, both yoghurts and honey. Cover and set aside in the refrigerator for 2 hours or overnight.

2. Add the fruit and almonds and serve.

Serves 6

Fruity Porridge

This is good old porridge with a fruity twist. Characteristic of dishes rich in whole grains, this warming breakfast will ward off the winter chills and keep you going until lunchtime. Serve with low-fat milk or calcium-enriched soy drink.

1¹/2 cups rolled oats

3 cups water

2 teaspoons honey

4 tablespoons chopped dried fruit such as prunes, apricots or raisins

1. Put the oats and water in a medium-sized saucepan and bring the mixture to the boil.

2. Reduce the heat, cover and cook over a low heat for 5–10 minutes, stirring every now and then.

3. Serve drizzled with the honey and sprinkled with the fruit.

Serves 2

Microwave Porridge

Porridge makes a great breakfast for the busiest of people, as single serves can be cooked very quickly in a microwave oven. The bonus is you are not left with a porridge-coated saucepan. Serve with low-fat milk or calcium-enriched soy drink.

3/4 cup quick-cooking oats

1¹/4 cups water

1–2 teaspoons honey

1. Place the oats and water in a heatproof serving bowl.

2. Cook on High for 1 minute, then stir, and cook for a further 30 seconds.

3. Remove from the microwave and serve drizzled with the honey.

Serves 1

Breakfast Pancakes (opposite)

Breakfast Pancakes

A great recipe for the weekend or holiday mornings when there is more time to enjoy these pancakes. Serve them straight from the pan spread with a little margarine. Or top them with sliced fresh bananas and kiwifruit, or strawberries, raspberries and blueberries, then drizzle with a little maple syrup or warm honey. Serve with plain or fruit yoghurt or with a fruit smoothie (page 69) or a lassi (page 89).

1¹/₂ cups wholemeal self-raising flour

1 cup untoasted muesli or rolled oats

1 teaspoon mixed spice

1 egg, beaten

1 tablespoon honey

2 cups low-fat milk

extra milk

3 teaspoons margarine

1. Combine the flour, muesli and spice in a bowl, then make a hollow in the middle.

2. Add the egg and honey to the hollow and, using a wooden spoon, gradually beat in the milk. Allow to stand for 30 minutes, if possible, to soften the flour and muesli (or oats). The mixture should be the consistency of a thick batter and, depending on the muesli used, you may need to stir in a little more milk.

3. Heat 1 teaspoon of the margarine in a frying pan over a medium to high heat. Use a large spoonful of the batter for each pancake, and cook the pancakes in batches, adding a little margarine to the pan as needed.

4. Cook the pancakes until golden brown, 1–2 minutes for each side. Keep the cooked pancakes warm on a plate covered with a clean dry tea towel until you are ready to serve them.

Makes about 12

Banana Spice Muffins

Catherine Saxelby has kindly provided the recipe for these lovely fruity muffins which are delicious served hot or cold. Enjoy them straight from the oven, or, for a quick breakfast, reheat them briefly in microwave oven and serve them with fresh fruit or a fruit smoothie.

½ **teaspoon margarine**

3 **large very ripe bananas**

3 **tablespoons brown sugar**

2 **tablespoons margarine**

3 **tablespoons honey**

½ **cup orange juice**

¼ **teaspoon bicarbonate of soda dissolved in 1 tablespoon hot water**

1 **egg, beaten**

1 **cup All Bran**

2 **teaspoons mixed spice**

1½ **cups wholemeal self-raising flour**

1. Preheat the oven to 200°C. Brush a muffin tray with the ½ teaspoon margarine.

2. Using a potato masher or a fork, mash the bananas with the sugar.

3. Place the margarine and the honey in a small saucepan and heat gently until the margarine melts, then add to the banana mixture.

4. Stir in the orange juice, bicarbonate of soda and water, egg, All Bran and mixed spice. Gradually stir in the flour, mixing only until the flour is incorporated. (Over mixing will cause the muffins to become tough.)

5. Spoon the mixture into the prepared tray and bake in the preheated oven until golden brown and cooked through, 15–20 minutes.

Makes 12

Mushroom Spinach Couscous with Chick Peas

This is a really tasty quick dish that can be whipped up and served on its own. It's also delicious served surrounded with roasted vegetables, so why not get some pumpkin or sweet potatoes roasting in the oven before you start . . .

1 tablespoon olive oil

1 large onion, chopped

350 g mushrooms, sliced

1 cup cooked or canned chick peas, drained

4 garlic cloves, crushed

1/2 bunch spinach, trimmed, washed and drained

2 cups couscous

1 cup vegetable stock

1 red capsicum, roasted (page 35) and sliced

cracked black pepper

1 large or 2 small lemons, cut into wedges

1. Heat the oil and stir-fry the onions over a high heat for 2 minutes. Reduce the heat and stir in the mushrooms and chick peas. Cover and cook over a low to medium heat for 10 minutes.

2. Add the garlic and spinach to the saucepan, stirring to combine well. Cover and cook over a medium heat until the spinach wilts, about 2 minutes.

3. Add the couscous and vegetable stock, and stir to combine. Remove from the heat, cover and set aside for 5 minutes to allow the couscous to absorb the stock.

4. Spoon the couscous onto serving plates. Top each serve with a clump of red capsicum strips. Dust with the pepper, arrange 2 lemon wedges on the side of each plate and serve at once.

Serves 4

Chicken, Tabouli & Nori Wraps (opposite)

Chicken, Tabouli & Nori Wraps

They're delicious, they're filling and they are the answer when you are tired of the usual sandwich fare.

4 sheets mountain bread

4 sheets nori

2 ripe avocados, sliced

2 red capsicums, roasted (page 35), sliced

4 tablespoons chopped sun-dried tomatoes

400 g cooked chicken, shredded

1 quantity Terrific Tabouli Salad (this page)

1. Put 1 sheet of mountain bread on a chopping board and top each one with a nori sheet. Scatter with the remaining ingredients in the order given.

2. Roll up the bread tightly and, if not serving at once, wrap in plastic and refrigerate until needed. Use a sharp knife to cut each roll into neat slices on the diagonal, to reveal the colourful filling.

Serves 4

Terrific tabouli Salad

Serve with barbecued or roasted meat or kebabs, or use as a sandwich filling.

1 cup cracked wheat (burghul)

2 large tomatoes, diced

1 white onion, finely diced

juice of 2 lemons

1 tablespoon olive oil

2 cups chopped parsley

2 tablespoons chopped mint

a few drops of Tabasco sauce

1. Place the wheat in a bowl, cover with water and set aside for 15 minutes. Pour the mixture into a coarse sieve and stir to remove all the water.

2. Combine the wheat with the remaining ingredients and serve at once.

Serves 4

Spinach & Pumpkin Lasagna

Luscious and light, this vegetable-packed lasagna is great teamed with a leafy green salad and fresh bread. It is best prepared several hours ahead of time, or the day before you need it. (This allows time for the flavours to mingle and the texture to become firm enough to cut it into neat slices.)

1 kg pumpkin, skin and seeds removed, chopped

150 g feta, chopped or crumbled

1 bunch spinach, trimmed and washed well

1 quantity Vegie Pasta Sauce (page 45), or 6 cups bottled pasta sauce

500 g fresh lasagna sheets

90 g parmesan, finely grated

1. Steam the pumpkin until tender, about 15 minutes. Mash roughly and stir in the feta.

2. Steam the spinach until just wilted, then chop roughly.

3. Preheat the oven to 190°C.

4. Assemble the lasagna in layers as follows: sauce, lasagna sheets, pumpkin and feta, lasagna sheets, sauce, lasagna sheets, spinach, lasagna sheets and sauce.

5. Bake in the preheated oven for 25 minutes, then sprinkle with parmesan and bake for a further 10 minutes. Remove from the oven and allow to stand for at least 10 minutes before slicing.

Serves 8–10

tips *The fresh spinach can be replaced with a 420 g packet of frozen spinach which has been thawed and chopped. (There is no need to steam it.)*

For a change, replace the feta cheese with 1/4 cup chopped roasted walnuts or pine nuts. (To roast nuts and seeds, see page 108.)

Stir-Fried Rice with Vegetables & Cashews

This is a quick and easy dish. Have fun varying this recipe by using other chopped or diced vegetables such as capsicums or celery, and try different types of rice, such as a mixture of brown rice cooked with a little wild rice.

1 tablespoon peanut oil

1 onion, chopped

2 garlic cloves, chopped

1 teaspoon finely sliced chillies, seeds removed

1 teaspoon grated ginger

1/2 bunch spring onions, sliced, green tops included

2 zucchini, trimmed and sliced

2 cups finely shredded cabbage or bok choy

1/2 cup cashew nuts

3 cups cold cooked rice

2 cups bean shoots

1 tablespoon salt-reduced soy sauce

1 teaspoon sesame oil (optional)

1. Heat the peanut oil in a large frying pan or wok and stir-fry the onion, garlic, chillies, ginger, spring onions, zucchini, cabbage and cashew nuts over a high heat for 10 minutes.

2. Add the rice and cook for 5 more minutes, stirring occasionally. Add the bean shoots and soy sauce and continue cooking, stirring, until all the vegetables are tender but still crisp, about 5 minutes.

3. Remove from the heat, stir in the sesame oil and serve at once.

Serves 4

ON OCCASION!

Replace the cashews with 1 cup of sliced lean ham or bacon.

Vegetable Pasta with Balsamic & Basil (opposite)

Vegetable Pasta with Balsamic & Basil

A light and tasty pasta, perfect for casual summer meals. Serve hot as it is, or cold as a salad with a generous squeeze of lemon juice. Shell or bow-tie pasta are especially suited to this recipe because they hold tiny pools of the balsamic vinegar.

500 g shell or bow-tie pasta

1 tablespoon olive oil

1 large or 2 medium-sized onions, diced

1 large capsicum, seeds removed and cut into strips

2 zucchini, cut into strips

6 garlic cloves, finely sliced

6 Roma tomatoes, halved lengthwise

1/2 cup shredded fresh basil leaves

125 g feta, crumbled or cut into strips

2 tablespoons balsamic vinegar

cracked black pepper

fresh basil leaves (garnish)

1. Put a large pan of water on the stove to boil and cook the pasta until *al dente*. Drain the pasta and set aside.

2. Meanwhile, heat the oil in a frying pan or large saucepan with a lid, and add the onions, capsicum, zucchini and garlic and stir over a high heat for 1 minute. Reduce the heat to low, cover and cook for 15 minutes, stirring occasionally.

3. Meanwhile, place the tomatoes, cut side down, on an oven tray and cook under a hot grill until the skins become blistered and charred. Remove from the heat and set aside until cool enough to handle, then slip off the skins.

4. Add the pasta and tomatoes to the vegetables and mix well over a medium heat. Remove from the heat and stir in the shredded basil and feta.

5. Sprinkle with balsamic vinegar, dust with the pepper and serve garnished with the fresh basil leaves.

Serves 4

Rice Volcanoes

The explosive sauce that lurks in the innocent-looking
indentations in the tops of these patties gives the dish its name.
If you're not quite ready for such a blast to your tastebuds,
simply use less chilli sauce. Rice Volcanoes make a lovely
light meal served with oven-roasted vegetables, steamed green
vegetables or a crisp salad. This recipe allows for leftovers
to be enjoyed the next day.

1/4 teaspoon olive oil

3 cups cooked and cooled
brown rice

1 small capsicum,
seeds removed, finely diced

1 onion, finely diced or
4 spring onions, finely sliced

1 small zucchini, finely diced

1 carrot, grated

2–3 ripe tomatoes, diced

1 cup grated tasty cheese

1/2 cup chopped parsley

about 1/2 cup wheat germ
or rice bran

2–3 teaspoons chilli sauce

1 quantity Roasted Red
Capsicum Sauce (page 35)

1. Preheat the oven to 200°C. Brush a baking tray
with the oil.

2. Combine the rice, vegetables, cheese and
parsley, then mix in enough wheat germ to reach
a soft dough consistency. (Use your hands – the
warmth will melt the cheese slightly and help hold
the mixture together.) Form the mixture into
about 12 cone-shaped patties, pressing the
mixture together firmly. Arrange them, thicker
end down, on the prepared baking tray.

4. Using the handle of a wooden spoon, make
a deep indentation in the centre of each patty.
Combine the chilli sauce with 1/4 cup of the
capsicum sauce and drop 1 teaspoonful of the
mixture into each indentation.

5. Bake in the preheated oven until golden brown,
25–30 minutes. Place the remaining capsicum
sauce in a small saucepan and gently reheat. To
serve, pour a little sauce onto each serving plate.
Arrange the rice volcanoes on top and spoon a
little of the capsicum sauce down the side of
each rice volcano.

Makes 12 (Pictured on page 11)

Vegie Wraps

These scrumptious wraps, which are bursting with flavour from the chilli jam, make a delightful light meal or a special snack.

4 sheets mountain bread

1/2 quantity Chilli Jam (this page)

1 carrot, cut into sticks

1 capsicum, seeds removed, cut into sticks

2 Lebanese cucumbers, cut into sticks

16 mint or basil leaves

1. Lay the mountain bread out flat on a benchtop and spread the chilli jam in a strip along the edge of the bread closest to you.

2. Lay the vegetables in a row on top of the chilli jam, then top with mint leaves. Roll up the bread firmly and, using a sharp knife, cut into neat slices.

3. Serve at once, or wrap the rolls in plastic wrap and keep in the refrigerator for 1 day.

Serves 4 *(Pictured on page 10)*

Chilli Jam

Adding soy beans to this scrumptious jam not only keeps the fat content low, it is a great way to enjoy more legumes!

1/2 cup dry roasted peanuts

1/2 cup drained canned soy beans

10 garlic cloves, chopped

2 teaspoons chopped chillies

1 tablespoon brown sugar

2 tomatoes, chopped

juice of 2 lemons

2 teaspoons salt-reduced soy sauce

a few drops of sesame oil

pepper

1. Using a blender or food processor, chop the peanuts and the soy beans roughly, then transfer the mixture to a small saucepan with the remaining ingredients, except for the sesame oil and pepper.

2. Bring the mixture to the boil over a medium heat. Reduce the heat, cover and simmer until thick, 15–20 minutes, stirring occasionally to prevent the mixture sticking to the pan.

3. Remove from the heat and stir in the sesame oil and pepper. If not using straightaway, store in a jar in the refrigerator for 2–3 days.

Serves 4 *(Pictured on page 10)*

This page: *Sesame Tuna Steaks* (page 39) with *Corn Salsa* (page 38)
Opposite: *Pumpkin Soup with Fish Dumplings* (page 32)

eat! enjoy!

Vegetables
& legumes

With their vibrant hues and fabulous flavours, vegetables and legumes are often the unsung heroes of a meal. Not any more! Here vegetables and legumes star as flavour-packed soups, salsas and salads and tasty main meals. They also feature as a colourful backdrop for meat, fish and poultry, and as a surprising ingredient for sweet muffins.

lentil Soup
with Roasted Capsicums

A delicious soup for late summer or autumn when capsicums and Roma tomatoes abound. Great served with your choice of bread. Why not try warmed Turkish bread for a change?

500 g Roma tomatoes, halved lengthwise

2 red capsicums, cut into 4, seeds removed

1 tablespoon olive oil

1 large onion, chopped

2 carrots, sliced or diced

3 cups cooked lentils

3 cups vegetable stock

1/2 cup chopped coriander or parsley or sliced spring onion tops

1 tablespoon sweet chilli sauce

pepper

1. Cook the tomatoes and capsicums in batches under a hot grill until the skins become blistered and charred. Place them in a plastic bag and turn the top over to keep the steam in. Set aside for 10 minutes until they are cool enough to handle.

2. Meanwhile, heat the oil in a large saucepan and stir-fry the onion and carrots over a high heat for 2 minutes. Reduce the heat, cover and cook over a low to medium heat for 5 minutes, stirring every now and then.

3. Add the lentils and stock and bring the soup to the boil, stirring occasionally.

4. Peel the capsicums and tomatoes and slice the flesh. Add to the soup and return it to the boil, stirring. Reduce the heat, then cover and cook over a low to medium heat until all the vegetables are tender, about 15 minutes. Stir in the coriander, sweet chilli sauce and pepper and serve piping hot.

Serves 4–6

tip *You can use cooked dried red or yellow split lentils, brown lentils or drained canned lentils.*

Chilli Pumpkin Soup with Chick Peas

A simple colourful soup that becomes a meal when served with plenty of warmed pita bread or crusty bread rolls, or ladled over a mound of freshly cooked couscous in soup plates. Butternut pumpkin retains its shape well even when tender, and creates a stunning colour contrast with the tomatoes.

1 tablespoon olive oil

1 large onion, chopped

500 g butternut pumpkin, skin and seeds removed

2 teaspoons sliced chillies, seeds removed

4 garlic cloves, chopped

2 teaspoons ground cumin

2 cups canned or cooked chick peas, drained

1 x 810 g can crushed tomatoes

2 cups vegetable stock

1/2 cup chopped coriander

cracked black pepper

1. Heat the oil in a large saucepan and stir-fry the onion over a high heat for 2 minutes. Reduce the heat, cover and cook over a low to medium heat for 5 minutes, stirring occasionally.

2. Meanwhile, cut the pumpkin into 2 cm cubes. Add the pumpkin, chillies, garlic and cumin to the onion, stirring. Cover and continue to cook over a low to medium heat for 5 minutes, stirring every now and then.

3. Add the chick peas, tomatoes and stock. Bring the soup to the boil then reduce the heat, cover and cook over a low to medium heat until the pumpkin is tender, about 15 minutes. Stir in the coriander and serve piping hot, dusted with the pepper.

Serves 4 *(Pictured on page 30)*

tip *TO COOK CHICK PEAS: Soak dried chick peas in double the amount of cold water for 1 day or overnight. Drain and transfer to a saucepan with double the amount of water. Bring to the boil and cook rapidly for 10 minutes. Reduce the heat and cook over a medium heat until tender, about 45 minutes. For 2 cups cooked chick peas, you will need 1 cup dried chick peas.*

This page: *Chilli Pumpkin Soup with Chick Peas* (page 29)
Opposite top: *Catch-of-the-Day Fish Soup* (page 97); bottom: *Spinach & Prawn Soup* (page 96)

Pumpkin Soup with Fish dumplings

This tasty soup is another delicious way to enjoy more fish.
Serve with sourdough bread.

200 g white fish fillets, cut into cubes

1 egg white

1 tablespoon cornflour

2 tablespoons sliced chives

1 tablespoon chopped coriander

1 tablespoon chopped parsley

2 tablespoons mirin or dry sherry

1 litre fish stock

½ cup white wine

300 g butternut pumpkin, peeled, seeds removed, cut into 1 cm cubes

1 tomato, sliced

fresh parsley, coriander or chives (garnish)

1. To make the dumplings, purée the fish in a blender, then transfer to a bowl. Combine thoroughly with the egg white, cornflour, chives, coriander, parsley and mirin. Working with 1 tablespoon of the mixture at a time, form into small dumplings and set aside.

2. Put the fish stock and wine into a large pan and bring to the boil. Reduce the heat so the stock is simmering. Drop the dumplings into the stock one at a time, and cook them until they rise to the surface, 3–5 minutes. Remove the dumplings with a slotted spoon, put in a heatproof bowl, cover and keep warm.

3. To make the soup, add the pumpkin to the stock and bring it to the boil. Reduce the heat, cover and cook over a medium heat until the pumpkin is tender, about 10 minutes.

4. Arrange the fish dumplings, tomato and pumpkin in a large soup tureen, or in deep individual bowls. Ladle the hot stock over, garnish with the herbs and serve at once.

Serves 4 *(Pictured on page 27)*

Risotto with Mediterranean Vegetables & Bok Choy

*This full-flavoured dish is perfect for a light meal on its own,
or serve with a salad of fresh ripe tomatoes and
crispy lettuce with crusty Italian bread on the side.*

2 tablespoons olive oil

3 cups short-grain rice

5 cups warm water

1/2 cup white wine

1 tablespoon olive oil (extra)

1 onion, diced

1 carrot, diced

3/4 eggplant, diced

6 sun-dried tomatoes, chopped

2 artichoke hearts, drained and diced

1/2 capsicum, seeds removed, diced

3 garlic cloves, chopped

1 baby bok choy, trimmed, washed and chopped

2 teaspoons balsamic vinegar

cracked black pepper

1. Heat the oil in a large frying pan and stir-fry the rice over a medium to high heat for 4 minutes. Add the water and wine and bring the mixture to the boil. Cover and cook over a low to medium heat for 10–12 minutes.

2. Meanwhile, heat the additional oil in a separate frying pan and stir-fry the onion, carrot, eggplant, sun-dried tomatoes, artichoke hearts, capsicum, garlic and bok choy over a high heat for 2–3 minutes. Reduce the heat, cover and cook for 8–10 minutes.

3. Stir the cooked vegetables through the rice. Season with the balsamic vinegar and the cracked black pepper and serve at once.

Serves 4–6

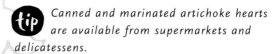 *Canned and marinated artichoke hearts are available from supermarkets and delicatessens.*

Geoff Jansz's
Italian autumn Salad

On his farm in Bowral, in the Southern Highlands of NSW, **Geoff Jansz** grows a variety of fruits and vegetables which he uses to pursue his passion for cooking with fresh seasonal ingredients. According to Geoff, food, and the pleasure it brings, is a wonderful way of bringing people together. Geoff shares this philosophy on Channel Nine's *What's Cooking*, and has written three books, *Taking the Freshest Approach*, *Favourite Recipes* and *Geoff Jansz Desserts*.

Geoff says 'As we celebrate the summer by cooling down at the beach, or warm up in winter in front of a log fire, celebrate the last of the autumn capsicums and tomatoes by making this salad.'

4 large slices sourdough bread or focaccia

1/3 cup olive oil

1 garlic clove, peeled and cut in half

1/2 cup balsamic vinegar

2 red capsicums, seeds removed, cut into thin strips

1 carrot, cut into thin strips

1 large onion, finely sliced

100 g lettuce leaves

200 g soft goat's cheese or feta or ricotta

1/4 cup small black olives

1 tablespoon small capers

1 tomato, diced

1. Brush the bread with a little of the oil, then cook it on a chargrill or in a preheated 210°C oven until lightly browned. Rub the cut garlic all over the bread to flavour it.

2. Place the remaining oil, vinegar, capsicums, carrot and onion in a frying pan and toss over a medium heat until hot.

3. Remove from the heat and allow to rest for 10 minutes before reheating. Repeat this heating and resting process five times to release the flavoursome juices from the vegetables.

4. Place a slice of bread on each serving plate and top with the lettuce. Reserving the cooking juices, remove the vegetables from the pan and arrange on the lettuce.

5. Blend the juices with the cheese until it resembles a mayonnaise, thinning with a little water if necessary. Drizzle the mixture over the salad, scatter with the olives, capers and tomatoes, and serve at once.

Serves 4

Roasted Capsicums

*With their tender slippery texture and sweet luscious flavour,
roasted capsicums are irresistible. Serve in strips as part of
an antipasto platter, or blend until smooth with flavourings
and stock, or yoghurt, to make delicious sauces. See Roasted
Red Capsicum Sauce (this page) and Roasted Capsicum
& Yoghurt Sauce (page 84).*

**2 capsicums, each cut into 4,
seeds removed**

1. Cook the capsicums under a hot grill until the
skins are blistered and charred. Put them in a
plastic bag, and set aside for 10 minutes to cool.

2. Remove the skins from the capsicums and
discard. Use the capsicums as required or store in
an airtight container in the refrigerator for 2–3 days.

Roasted Red Capsicum Sauce

*A really delicious light and bright sauce that adds flavour and
colour to a host of dishes.*

**2 red capsicums, roasted
(this page)**

2 garlic cloves, crushed

**¹/₂ cup vegetable stock or
tomato juice**

2 teaspoons balsamic vinegar

a few drops of Tabasco sauce

Blend the capsicums with the garlic, vegetable
stock or juice, balsamic vinegar and Tabasco
until smooth. For a thinner sauce, add a little
more stock or juice.

Serves 4 *(Pictured on back cover flap)*

Hey Pesto!

Pesto is famous for adding verve to pasta, but don't stop there! Pesto can be added to soups, stews, dressings and sandwiches to tantalise jaded tastebuds. If not using at once, store in the refrigerator for up to a week or freeze it in containers and defrost it as needed. Freshly prepared pesto has a far superior flavour to bottled pesto (available at larger supermarkets and delicatessens) but keep a supply of bottled pesto in the pantry for convenience.

Sweet Basil Pesto

3 cups sweet basil leaves

3 tablespoons extra-virgin olive oil

10 garlic cloves

1/4 teaspoon pepper

30 g hazel or pine nuts

Blend all the ingredients together until the desired texture.

Serves 8

Semi-Dried tomato Pesto

100 g semi-dried tomatoes

3 tablespoons extra-virgin olive oil

10 garlic cloves

1 tablespoon tomato paste

30 g macadamia or pine nuts

Blend all the ingredients together until the desired texture.

Serves 8

Macadamia Chilli Ginger Pesto

Sweet and hot, this pesto is wonderful served on freshly cooked noodles or vegetables such as stir-fried baby bok choy.

6 red Mexican chillies, seeds removed, roughly chopped

1 cup parsley leaves

60 g macadamias, roasted (page 108) and cooled

10 garlic cloves

40 g glacé ginger

3 tablespoons macadamia oil

Blend all the ingredients together until the desired texture.

Serves 8

 Replace the parsley with coriander for a tasty variation.

Pesto Dipping Sauce

Delicious served with finger foods such as filo rolls or a platter of fresh and blanched (see tip) vegetables.

2 tablespoons pesto of your choice

2 teaspoons balsamic vinegar

1/2 cup fresh or canned tomato purée

a few drops of Tabasco sauce

pepper

Combine all the ingredients together in a small bowl and, if not using at once, store in a screw-topped jar in the refrigerator for 2–3 days.

Serves 8

TO BLANCH VEGETABLES: Place them in a deep heatproof bowl. Cover with boiling water and allow to stand for 30–60 seconds. Drain the vegetables, then rinse them under cold water to prevent further cooking.

Super Salsas

Salsas are mixtures of freshly prepared vegetables or fruits pepped up with herbs, spices and lemon or lime juice. They are great for adding a burst of colour and flavour to pasta, soups, stews, patties or burgers and sandwiches.

Avocado & Coriander Salsa

This is fabulous served with hot and spicy dishes.

1 large avocado, diced

juice of 1 lemon or lime

2 tablespoons coriander leaves

cracked black pepper

2 tablespoons diced red onion

Combine all the ingredients and serve as soon as possible. This is best served fresh, but if not using at once, store in an airtight container in the refrigerator for up to 1 day.

Serves 4 *(Pictured on front cover flap)*

Corn Salsa

A quick and tasty salsa to serve with barbecued meat, fish, poultry or tofu. It also makes a colourful garnish for piping hot thick soups.

1 cup sweetcorn kernels

1 small onion, finely diced

1 tomato, finely diced

2 tablespoons sweet chilli sauce

2 tablespoons chopped coriander

juice of ½ lime or lemon

pepper

Combine all the ingredients. If not serving at once, store in an airtight container in the refrigerator for 1–2 days.

Serves 4 *(Pictured on page 26)*

 tip *You can use fresh, frozen or drained canned sweetcorn kernels.*

Carnival Capsicum Salsa

Zesty, colourful and so, so easy, this salsa is fabulous for spooning on top of piping hot thick soups, pasta or couscous.

1 red capsicum, seeds removed, finely diced

1 yellow or green capsicum, seeds removed, finely diced

1–2 teaspoons sliced chillies, seeds removed

2 spring onions, finely sliced, green tops included

2 garlic cloves, chopped

juice of 1 lemon or lime

cracked black pepper

Combine all the ingredients and serve as soon as possible. This is best served fresh, but if not using at once, store in an airtight container in the refrigerator for 1–2 days.

Serves 4 *(Pictured on front cover flap)*

Sesame tuna Steaks with Salsa

A quick to cook and easy to eat dish that is especially delicious served with steamed asparagus and mashed sweet potatoes. Try these scrumptious steaks with one of the salsas featured here, or with Pineapple Mint Salsa (page 55) or Citrus Salsa (page 59).

1 tablespoon olive oil

4 tuna steaks (about 600 g)

1/2 cup sesame seeds, roasted (page 108)

1 lime, cut into thin wedges

1 quantity salsa of your choice

1. Heat the oil in a frying pan and cook the tuna quickly over a medium to high heat until medium to rare.

2. Spread the seeds out on a plate and coat the steaks with the seeds. Serve at once with the lime wedges and salsa alongside.

Serves 4 *(Pictured on page 26)*

Vegetable Chicken Kebabs

*Light, bright and luscious, this dish is especially good served on
a bed of Yellow Lentil Mash (this page).*

1 cup plain skim-milk yoghurt

1 tablespoon lemon juice

1 tablespoon ground cumin

3 garlic cloves, crushed

500 g skinless chicken breast
fillets, cut into 2 cm cubes

8 button mushrooms

1 capsicum, seeds removed,
cut into 2 cm squares

1 onion, cut into 2 cm squares

8 bamboo skewers, presoaked
in water for 30 minutes

4 lemon wedges

1. Combine the yoghurt, lemon juice, cumin and garlic in a bowl. Toss the chicken in the mixture until it is evenly coated.

2. Cover and set aside to marinate in the refrigerator for at least 1 hour.

3. Thread the chicken onto the skewers alternatively with the vegetables, then cook them under a hot grill or on a hot barbecue until golden brown and cooked through, 5–6 minutes on each side.

4. Serve with the lemon wedges.

Serves 4

Yellow Lentil Mash

This is a great alternative to the usual vegetables.

1 tablespoon olive oil

1 onion, chopped

2 cups yellow split lentils
(channa dahl)

4 cups water

pepper

2 teaspoons salt-reduced soy
sauce

1. Heat the oil in a saucepan and stir-fry the onion over a high heat for 1 minute. Add the lentils and water and bring to the boil. Reduce the heat, cover and cook over a medium heat until the lentils are tender, 30–35 minutes, stirring occasionally.

2. Season with the pepper and soy sauce and serve.

Serves 4

Michele Curtis' & Allan Campion's
Salad of Char Siew

Allan Campion and **Michele Curtis** are Melbourne-based food writers and chefs. They have co-authored many books, including *Tucker for Tots*, *The Goods: Melbourne's best food shops*, and *Chilli Jam: Choosing and using Asian ingredients*. Together with graphic designer Ian Scott they run Purple Egg Publishing, which compiles the *Seasonal Produce Diary*. This year Purple Egg launched *Chalk and Cheese*, Will Studd's comprehensive book on Australian cheese.

100 g snowpea shoots

100 g tatsoi leaves

1 small bunch baby bok choy, thinly sliced

1/4 Chinese cabbage (wong nga bak), thinly sliced

1/2 cup coriander leaves

100 g green papaya (pawpaw), peeled, seeds removed, shredded

1 carrot, shredded

100 g bean shoots

1/3 cup dry-roasted peanuts, chopped

250 g char siew, thinly sliced

2 spring onions, finely sliced

LIME & SESAME DRESSING

juice of 1 lime

1 tablespoon fish sauce

1/2 teaspoon sesame oil

50 ml peanut oil

1. Mix the snowpea shoots, tatsoi leaves, baby bok choy, Chinese cabbage and coriander leaves and arrange on a platter.

2. For the dressing, combine all the ingredients. (Use within 1–2 hours to retain the fresh lime flavour.)

3. Combine the papaya, carrot, bean shoots, peanuts and pork in a large bowl, then arrange on the greens. Top with the spring onions, drizzle with the dressing and serve.

Serves 4–6

 Asian greens make a wonderful base for all salads and are available from Asian grocers and market stalls.

Tatsoi is a tender-leafed Asian green.

Char siew is a marinated roast pork available from Chinese bake houses.

Kumera & Cashew Patties

Light and tasty, these patties are dotted with roasted cashews which provide a lovely texture. Serve topped with a dollop of Mango Chilli Jam (page 55), with warmed tortillas or souvlaki bread and a salad of mixed greens alongside.

300 g firm tofu, drained

½ cup raw cashew nuts, roasted (page 108)

200 g kumera, peeled and grated

3 spring onions, finely sliced, green tops included

2 garlic cloves, crushed

2–3 teaspoons sweet chilli sauce

4 tablespoons chick pea flour (besan flour)

2 tablespoons olive oil

1 quantity Mango Chilli Jam (page 55)

1. Combine all the ingredients except for the oil and chilli jam (the mixture should be the consistency of a soft dough).

2. Form the mixture into 12 patties.

3. Heat 1 tablespoon of the oil in a frying pan and cook 6 of the patties over a medium to high heat until golden brown, about 2–3 minutes on each side. Add the remaining oil and cook the rest of the patties in the same way.

Makes about 12 *(Pictured on page 54)*

Garlic Roasted Vegetables

*The aroma of roasted vegetables brings back memories of
childhood. Not many people would say no to crisp golden brown
roast potatoes. But vegetables don't have to be cooked in a bath
of dripping to be tasty. Roasting them brushed with olive oil with
a touch of garlic and black pepper adds a whole new dimension.*

1 tablespoon olive oil

2–3 garlic cloves, chopped

500 g kumera, peeled and cut
into neat pieces

500 g pumpkin, peeled,
seeds removed and cut into
neat pieces

4 medium-sized potatoes,
scrubbed or peeled and
quartered

4–6 large cap or medium-
sized field mushrooms,
stalks removed

4–6 Roma tomatoes,
halved lengthwise

cracked black pepper

1. Preheat the oven to 200°C. Brush 3 baking
trays with a little of the oil.

2. Combine the remaining oil with the chopped
garlic. Place the kumera, pumpkin and potatoes
in a large bowl with the garlic oil, and, using your
hands, toss the vegetables so they become
evenly coated with oil.

3. Arrange the kumera, pumpkin and potatoes
on 2 of the baking trays. Sprinkle with a little of
the cracked black pepper and bake in the
preheated oven until tender and lightly browned,
25–30 minutes.

4. Meanwhile, add the mushrooms and
tomatoes to the bowl the vegetables have been
mixed in. (It should contain a little olive oil and
garlic.) Toss them in the oil and arrange them on
the third baking tray. Sprinkle with the pepper
and bake in the preheated oven until tender,
15–20 minutes.

Serves 4–6

tip *It's well worthwhile roasting lots more
vegetables than you need for a meal.
Roasted vegetables are delicious served as salads
or added to antipasto platters, risotto, soups
and stews.*

Roasted Pumpkin & Beetroot salad

A delicious colourful winter salad dressed with the robust flavour of extra-virgin olive oil, garlic and balsamic vinegar. Serve warm or cold with wedges of baked ricotta (see glossary) or feta cheese and crusty bread.

1 tablespoon olive oil

1 garlic clove, crushed

500 g pumpkin, peeled, seeds removed, cut into 2 cm cubes

500 g beetroot, peeled, cut into 1 cm wedges

1 Spanish onion, cut into thin wedges

cracked black pepper

1/2 cup basil or Italian parsley leaves

BALSAMIC DRESSING

11/2 tablespoons extra-virgin olive oil

1 tablespoon balsamic vinegar

1 tablespoon lemon or orange juice

1 teaspoon honey

2 garlic cloves, chopped finely

1. Preheat the oven to 200°C. Brush 1 or 2 baking trays with a little of the oil.

2. Combine the remaining oil with the garlic. Place the pumpkin, beetroot and onion in a large bowl and add the garlic oil. Toss the vegetables so that they become evenly coated with the oil.

3. Arrange the vegetables on the baking tray/s and sprinkle with the pepper. Bake in the preheated oven until tender and lightly browned, about 30 minutes. Remove from the oven and set aside to cool to room temperature, then transfer the vegetables to a bowl.

4. For the dressing, whisk all the ingredients together in a cup or small bowl with a fork, then drizzle over the vegetables.

5. Decorate with the basil (or parsley) and serve.

Serves 4 *(Pictured on back cover)*

PURPLE BLAZE

This sweet, tangy and spicy concoction is great served with pasta, grilled or roasted meat, filo parcels, patties, couscous and polenta.

2–3 teaspoons olive oil

1 onion, chopped

1 apple, cored and finely diced

1 teaspoon chopped chillies

1 x 425 g can tomatoes

2 garlic cloves, crushed

1/4 small red cabbage, shredded

1/4 cup currants

juice of 1 lemon

1. Heat the oil in a medium-sized saucepan and stir-fry the onion and apple over a high heat for 2 minutes. Add the remaining ingredients and bring the mixture to the boil, stirring occasionally.

2. Reduce the heat, cover and simmer until the cabbage is tender, about 15 minutes.

Serves 4

tip *The lemon juice, tomatoes, vinegar and other 'acidic' ingredients bring out the intense colour and flavour of red cabbage.*

Vegie Pasta Sauce

This recipe makes a large amount of tasty sauce – leftovers can be stored in the refrigerator and used in countless ways during the week.

1 tablespoon olive oil

1 large onion, chopped

1 capsicum, seeds removed, chopped

4 garlic cloves, crushed

2 stalks celery, chopped

2 x 810 g cans tomatoes

1/2 cup shredded basil leaves or 2 teaspoons dried basil

pepper

1. Heat the oil in a large saucepan and stir-fry the onion, capsicum, garlic and celery over a high heat for 1–2 minutes. Reduce the heat, cover and cook over a low to medium heat for 10 minutes, stirring every now and then.

2. Stir in the tomatoes and cook over a medium heat for 15 minutes, stirring occasionally to prevent the sauce from sticking to the pan. Add the basil, season with the pepper and serve.

Serves 8–10

Hot & Spicy New Potatoes

If you are a potato lover, you will find these irresistible.

12 very small new potatoes

1 tablespoon olive oil

1 teaspoon medium–hot curry powder

1 tablespoon finely chopped onions

1/2 cup water

1 tablespoon Worcestershire sauce

2 tablespoons chopped parsley or coriander

1. Steam or boil the potatoes until just tender but still firm, about 15 minutes. To cook in a microwave oven, prick the skins with a fork, then place in a microwave ovenproof dish, cover and cook on high for 10–12 minutes.

2. Meanwhile, heat the oil in a frying pan, add the curry powder and onions and stir over a low heat until the onion is soft, 2–3 minutes. Stir in the water and Worcestershire sauce and bring to the boil.

3. Add the cooked potatoes and toss over a low heat until the potatoes are piping hot and the liquid has evaporated. Sprinkle with the parsley and serve.

Serves 4

Carrot Parsnip Mash

1 medium-sized onion, diced

3 large carrots, peeled and roughly chopped

3 large parsnips, peeled and roughly chopped

2 garlic cloves, crushed

a little milk

1. Put the onion, carrots, parsnips and garlic into a large saucepan with 1 1/2 cups water and cook until the vegetables are tender, about 30 minutes.

2. Alternatively, place the vegetables in a microwave ovenproof dish. Add 1/2 cup water, cover and cook on High until the vegetables are tender, about 20 minutes.

3. Drain any cooking liquid and mash the vegetables coarsely, adding a little milk to moisten if necessary. Cover and keep warm until required.

Serves 4

Quick Greens

Long gone are the overcooked soggy greens of the past – treat greens with respect and you will have completely different vegetables. The trick to ending up with vibrant tasty greens is to cook them quickly.

2–3 teaspoons olive oil

1/2 bunch spring onions, sliced, green tops included

250 g Brussels sprouts, trimmed and finely sliced

1 large or 2 small leeks, trimmed and finely sliced

1 cup green peas

1/4 cup vegetable stock

pepper

1. Heat the oil in a large saucepan and stir-fry the spring onions over a high heat for 1 minute. Add the Brussels sprouts, leek and peas and continue to cook over a high heat, stirring, for 2 minutes.

2. Remove from the heat and stir in the vegetable stock. Return the pan to the stove, cover and cook over a medium heat until the vegetables are still bright green yet tender, about 5 minutes. Season with the pepper and serve at once.

Serves 4

Quick Vegie Couscous

This easy dish is lovely served hot as an accompaniment to saucy dishes, or cold as a salad with a generous squeeze of lemon juice.

2 teaspoons olive oil

1 onion, chopped

1/4 cup slivered almonds

2 cups vegetables such as diced carrots and green peas

3 tablespoons dried currants

2 cups couscous

11/2 cups vegetable stock or water

1. Heat the oil in a saucepan and stir-fry the onion over a high heat for 1 minute. Add the almonds, vegetables and currants, stirring for 1 minute.

2. Reduce the heat, cover and cook until the vegetables are tender, about 5 minutes. Add the couscous and cook, stirring, over a medium heat for 2 minutes.

3. Add the stock, stir briefly, then remove from the heat and set aside for 5 minutes. Fluff up the couscous and vegetables with a fork, then serve.

Serves 4 *(Pictured on page 134)*

Zucchini Spice Muffins

Here, zucchini are successfully incorporated into muffins the same way carrots have been used to make tasty moist cakes for many years. This recipe comes in handy in summer when zucchini are prolific.

100 g margarine

¼ cup brown sugar

3 tablespoons honey

1 tablespoon mixed spice

2 teaspoons ground cinnamon

1 egg, lightly beaten

1 cup sultanas

2 cups grated zucchini

2 cups wholemeal self-raising flour

½ cup milk

1. Preheat the oven to 200°C. Brush a muffin tray with 1 teaspoon of the margarine.

2. Using a wooden spoon, combine the remaining margarine with the sugar, honey, mixed spice and cinnamon, beating until creamy.

3. Add the egg and beat well, then stir in the sultanas and zucchini. Fold in the flour alternately with the milk.

4. Spoon the mixture into the prepared tray and bake in the preheated oven until the muffins are cooked and brown, 20–25 minutes.

Makes 12

ON occasion!

Serve with a dollop of cream cheese that has been combined with a little mild-flavoured honey and finely grated lemon zest.

Choc o' Beet Muffins

Sounds offbeat, but there's nothing off about this liaison! Albeit unlikely partners, the chocolate and beetroot in this recipe pair up to produce surprisingly moist, delicious, rich-coloured muffins.

100 g margarine

1/2 cup dark brown sugar

1 egg, lightly beaten

1/2 cup cocoa

1 teaspoon vanilla extract

2 beetroot (about 500 g), cooked (see below) and coarsely grated

2 cups self-raising flour

3/4 cup milk

1. Preheat the oven to 200°C. Brush a muffin tray with 1 teaspoon of the margarine.

2. Using a wooden spoon, combine the remaining margarine with the sugar, beating until creamy. Add the egg and beat well. Stir in the cocoa, then the beetroot and vanilla. Fold the flour into the mixture alternately with the milk.

3. Spoon the mixture into the prepared tray and bake in the preheated oven until the muffins are cooked and brown, 20–25 minutes.

Serves 4

tip *TO COOK BEETROOT: Wash the beetroot thoroughly and leave the skin on. If the leaves are still attached, cut them off, leaving 1 cm of the stalks. Place the beetroot in a saucepan and just cover with water. Cover the pan and bring the water to the boil. Reduce the heat and cook the beetroot over a medium heat for 40–50 minutes until tender. Remove from the stove and drain. When cool enough to handle, slip the skins off the beetroot.*

This page: *Strawberry Refresher* (page 52)
Opposite: *Cantaloupe with Orange Sherbet* (page 61)

eat! enjoy!

Fruits

Fresh fruits are truly inspiring — who can forget the sensual shape of a pear
or the luscious flesh and seductive perfume of a perfectly ripe peach?

Even when the winter months are taking their toll we can revive the memories of
summer by turning to berries frozen at their peak goodness
and summer fruits canned in their own juice.

We can even reminisce as we savour the sweetness of dried fruits . . .

Strawberry Refresher

Serve this lovely chilled soup at the start of the meal during summer when strawberries are ripe and luscious and full of flavour. This is a great recipe for Christmas dinner when you want a light and delicious prelude to the main course. For special occasions, this soup looks stunning served in glass bowls propped in larger bowls of ice, or in shallow white soup bowls.

2 cups weak green tea

3 tablespoons sugar

finely grated zest and the juice of 1 lemon

2 tablespoons arrowroot, mixed to a paste with 1/4 cup cold water

1 cup orange juice

1 cup fruity white wine such as riesling

2 punnets ripe strawberries, hulled, mashed with a fork

4 sprigs mint or lemon verbena (garnish)

1. Combine the green tea, sugar, lemon zest and juice and bring to the boil.

2. Remove the pan from the heat and stir in the arrowroot paste. Return to the heat and cook, stirring until thickened, about 1 minute.

3. Stir in the orange juice, wine and strawberries and heat gently, stirring, for 2–3 minutes only.

4. Remove from the heat and allow to cool. Chill well before serving. Garnish with the mint.

Serves 4–6 *(Pictured on page 50)*

tips *The strawberries should retain some texture but if you prefer a smoother consistency, purée the mixture in a food processor or blender before chilling.*

Green tea is available at larger supermarkets and Asian grocery stores.

When serving chilled soups, first chill the serving bowls to ensure the soup is really cold.

Dynamic Dips

Try these simple ideas and then experiment with your own.
Serve with wedges of pita bread and crackers with a plate
of fresh and blanched (page 37) vegetables alongside.

Orange & tandoori yoghurt Dip

1 orange

1 cup plain skim-milk yoghurt

1 tablespoon tandoori paste

2 spring onions, finely chopped

1. Finely grate the zest of the orange. Peel the orange, then dice the flesh, removing any pips.

2. Combine the orange zest and flesh with the remaining ingredients. Chill well before serving.

Serves 4 *(Pictured on back cover flap)*

Beetroot, Mandarin & Horseradish Dip

125 g reduced-fat cream cheese e.g Light Philly cheese

1 cup plain skim-milk yoghurt

1 teaspoon dried dill

2 tablespoons horseradish sauce

2–3 tablespoons shredded canned beetroot, drained

1 x 200 g can mandarins, drained and chopped

1. Using a wooden spoon, soften the cream cheese, then beat it with the yoghurt, dill and horseradish sauce until smooth.

2. Fold in the beetroot and mandarin, cover and chill before serving.

Serves 4 *(Pictured on back cover flap)*

Kumera & Cashew Patties (page 42) with Mango Chilli Jam (opposite)

Mango chilli jam

A real tutti-frutti relish, perfect for barbecues and outdoor eating.
Serve with barbecued meat, fish or poultry or patties such as
Kumera & Cashew Patties (page 42).

2 mangoes, peeled and chopped

2 spring onions, finely sliced, green tops included

6 garlic cloves, chopped

1 tablespoon finely sliced chillies, seeds removed

2–3 teaspoons grated ginger

juice of 1 lemon

1 tablespoon brown sugar

cracked black pepper

1. Place all the ingredients in a small to medium-sized saucepan and bring the mixture to the boil. Reduce the heat, cover and simmer for 15–20 minutes or until thick, stirring occasionally.

2. If not using straightaway, store in a jar in the refrigerator for 2–3 days.

Serves 4

Pineapple mint salsa

A tasty salsa to serve with savoury and sweet dishes.

2 cups diced fresh ripe pineapple

3 tablespoons lemon juice

2 teaspoons sugar

2.5 cm piece fresh ginger, peeled and cut into thin strips

2 tablespoons shredded mint leaves

Put the pineapple, lemon juice, sugar and ginger into a small saucepan and cook until the pineapple softens slightly, 4–5 minutes. Remove from the heat and set aside to cool, then stir through the mint.

Serves 4

Poached Plums

Poaching is a lovely way to cook stone fruits such as plums. For red-fleshed plums, use dark grape juice to enhance the colour. For golden-fleshed plums, nectarines or apricots, use orange and mango juice or apple juice.

1½ cups fruit juice

2–3 tablespoons honey or soft brown sugar

1 cinnamon stick, snapped into three

8 plums, left whole or halved

1. Place the fruit juice, honey and cinnamon stick in a medium-sized saucepan and bring the mixture almost to the boil.

2. Reduce the heat and add the plums. Cover and cook the plums over a very low heat until they are just tender, but still retain their shape, 10–15 minutes, depending on the ripeness of the plums.

3. Remove the plums from the liquid and set aside.

4. Return the liquid to the stove and bring it to the boil. Reduce the heat and simmer until the liquid becomes quite syrupy, about 10 minutes.

5. Serve the plums with the cooking liquid spooned over.

Serves 4

Stewed Rhubarb

It is hard to go past good old stewed rhubarb! Its distinctive flavour – tart and sweet at the same time – makes it a beautiful topping for breakfast cereal. It can also be mixed with thick plain yoghurt or chilled Creamy No Stick Custard (page 88) for a refreshing light dessert.

1 bunch rhubarb, trimmed and cut into 2 cm pieces

⅓ cup mild-flavoured honey

juice of 1 lemon

Place all the ingredients in a saucepan, cover and bring to the boil. Reduce the heat and cook over a low to medium heat until the rhubarb is tender, about 10–15 minutes.

Serves 4

Baked Figs & Raspberries

A delicious celebration of Autumn fruits.

1/4 teaspoon mild-flavoured oil

8 figs, halved lengthwise

250 g seedless red grapes

2 tablespoons maple syrup

2 tablespoons honey

1/2 cup orange juice

1 teaspoon ground cinnamon

200 g raspberries

mint sprigs (garnish)

1. Preheat the oven to 180°C. Brush an ovenproof dish with the oil.

2. Place the figs cut side down in the prepared dish. Scatter the grapes around.

3. Combine the maple syrup, honey, orange juice and cinnamon and drizzle over the fruit. Cover and bake in the preheated oven for 30 minutes.

4. Arrange the figs and grapes on serving plates.

5. Combine the raspberries with the cooking juices and spoon the mixture around the figs and grapes. Serve garnished with mint sprigs.

Serves 4

Maple Berry Sauce

200 g fresh or frozen raspberries

4 tablespoons pure maple syrup

1. If using frozen berries make sure you remove them from the freezer at least 1 hour before using, or defrost them in a microwave oven.

2. Combine the raspberries with the maple syrup, then push the mixture though a coarse sieve to remove the pips. If not using at once, store in the refrigerator for 1–2 days.

Serves 4 *(Pictured on page 62)*

ON occasion!

Pour this beautiful sauce onto serving plates, top with slices of your favourite chocolate cake and serve scattered with even more berries.

Banana Brûlée with *Citrus Salsa* (opposite)

Banana Brûlée

*These bananas are simply delicious served with a dollop of plain
yoghurt. For a stunning dessert, serve on a bed of Citrus Salsa
(this page) which complements the caramelised bananas beautifully.*

2 large firm bananas

2 tablespoons lime or
lemon juice

4 tablespoons brown sugar

mint sprigs (garnish)

1. Preheat the grill to high.

2. Peel the bananas, then cut each one in half
crosswise. Cut each piece in half lengthwise so
you end up with 8 portions. Arrange the banana
slices on a foil-lined grill tray, brush with the lime
juice and sprinkle with the sugar. Preheat the
griller and cook under the hot grill until the sugar
caramelises, 2–3 minutes. Set aside for 1 minute.

3. Arrange the bananas on serving plates and
serve at once.

Serves 4

Citrus Salsa

*A refreshing fruity salsa, with lovely sunset hues, a tangy flavour
and an interesting crunch from the almonds.*

2 Navel oranges

350 g firm ripe pawpaw,
peeled and seeds removed

1 tablespoon brown sugar

1 tablespoon lime or lemon
juice

1/3 cup slivered almonds,
roasted (see page 108)

1. Peel the oranges, removing all the white pith.
Cut into segments, then cut each segment in
half. Put the oranges into a bowl.

2. Cut the pawpaw into 2 cm dice and add to the
oranges. Carefully stir through the brown sugar
and lime juice. Cover and chill. Just before
serving, fold through the roasted almonds.

Serves 4 *(Also pictured on front cover flap)*

TONY KHAN'S
Apple Berry Strudel

Executive Chef at La Brasserie restaurant in Melbourne, **Tony Khan** is well known for his eclectic style of cuisine. His exciting and dynamic repertoire includes French, Mediterranean and Asian cuisines. Tony also has a special interest in Kosher, vegetarian and lighter, healthier cooking. He firmly believes that presenting food should be an expression of the heart. Tony began his training in Singapore before working in some of the most prestigious hotels and restaurants in Australia and overseas.

Tony says, 'Apple Berry Strudel is not only delicious, it is quick and simple to prepare and contains no added sugar.'

1/4 **teaspoon mild-flavoured oil**

2 cups canned unsweetened pie apples, drained

3 tablespoons fresh breadcrumbs (see glossary)

1 teaspoon ground cinnamon

1 cup blueberries

1 cup strawberries

1/2 **cup sultanas**

4 sheets filo pastry

2 teaspoons oil

1 egg yolk, beaten

1. Preheat the oven to 190°C. Brush a baking tray with the 1/4 teaspoon oil.

2. Combine the apples, breadcrumbs, cinnamon, berries and sultanas.

3. Lay two sheets of the pastry on the bench and brush with 1 teaspoon of the oil. Top with another 2 sheets of pastry and brush with the rest of the oil.

4. Arrange the fruit mixture in a row along the long edge of the pastry, extending right to the edges. Carefully roll the fruit up in the pastry.

5. Place the strudel on the prepared tray, seam side down. Brush the pastry with the egg yolk, then, using a sharp knife, score the top of the strudel at intervals.

6. Bake in the preheated oven until golden brown, 12–15 minutes.

Serves 4–6

Cantaloupe with Orange Sherbet

A lovely light sweet for summer when cantaloupes are at their best.

500 g smooth ricotta

1 cup plain skim-milk yoghurt

1/2 cup mild-flavoured honey

1 tablespoon finely grated orange zest

1 cup fresh orange juice

1/2 cup skim-milk powder

1 small cantaloupe

8 sprigs mint

1. Blend the ricotta, yoghurt, honey, orange zest and juice and milk powder. Pour the mixture into a terrine dish or freezer container and freeze for at least 4 hours.

2. Just before serving, cut the cantaloupe into thick slices and remove the seeds. Arrange the cantaloupe slices on serving plates.

3. Remove the sherbet from the freezer and allow to stand at room temperature for 5 minutes.

4. Turn the sherbet out of the dish onto a chopping board. Using a large sharp knife, cut into slices, then cut the slices into triangles.

5. Top each serve of cantaloupe with triangles of sherbet and decorate with a mint sprig. Serve at once.

Serves 8 *(Pictured on page 51)*

Cherry Yoghurt Freezes (opposite) with *Maple Berry Sauce* (page 57) and *Cherry Yoghurt Thick Shakes* (opposite)

Cherry Yoghurt Freezes

These are simply yummy, and make great snacks to cool you down on hot summer days. For a special dessert, serve them with wedges of watermelon atop a pool of Maple Berry Sauce (page 57).

1/2 teaspoon mild-flavoured oil

250 g cherries, halved and pips removed

2 1/2 cups plain skim-milk yoghurt

4 tablespoons plum and raspberry jam

extra cherries (garnish)

1. Brush a muffin tray with the oil.

2. Combine the cherries, yoghurt and jam in a jug with a wooden spoon, then pour the mixture into the prepared muffin tray and freeze for at least 4 hours.

3. Remove from the freezer 5 minutes before required. Using a knife, loosen the freezes around the edges, then flip them out of the tray.

4. Serve on a small plate decorated with the extra cherries. They look great served as they are, but they look particularly stunning cut in half or into quarters to reveal the cherries inside.

Makes 10–12

Cherry Yoghurt thick Shakes

Thick and icy, and much lower in fat and sugar than the fast food variety!

4 Cherry Yoghurt Freezes (this page)

1 1/2 cups low-fat milk

1. Using a large sharp knife, cut each of the cherry yoghurt freezes into 4 pieces.

2. Using a blender, blend the freezes with the milk and serve at once, with a spoon for scooping.

Serves 2

Gabriel Gaté's
Pear & Prune Loaf

Gabriel Gaté's love of food and cooking, together with his outstanding skills as a chef and television presenter have greatly influenced the way Australians cook today. Gabriel has become a familiar face to television viewers and he currently presents a weekly segment with Bert Newton on *Good Morning Australia*. Gabriel has written thirteen cookbooks. The latest, *Good Food for Men,* received an Australian Food Writers' award and first prize at the International Cookbook Fair in Périgeux, France.

There is no added sugar or fat in this loaf –
the sweetness and moisture of the dried fruits are enough.

½ **teaspoon soft margarine**

10 **dried pear halves**

10 **dried apricots**

20 **dried pitted prunes**

4 **dried apple rings, halved**

2 **cups water**

1 **large banana**

1 **cup wholemeal self-raising flour**

½ **cup almond meal**

¼ **teaspoon ground cinnamon**

1 **teaspoon finely grated orange zest**

1. Preheat the oven to 180°C. Brush the margarine over the inside of a 20 cm loaf tin.

2. Place the pears, apricots, prunes, apple rings and water in a saucepan and bring to the boil. Reduce the heat, cover and cook over a low to medium heat for 5 minutes. Remove from the heat and, using a slotted spoon, remove the pears and prunes from the saucepan and set aside.

3. Blend the apricots and apples with the cooking liquid and banana, then transfer the mixture to a large mixing bowl.

4. Stir in the flour, almond meal, cinnamon and orange rind, then spoon about a quarter of the mixture into the prepared tin.

5. Top with half of the pears, then layer with another quarter of the cake mixture. Top with a layer of prunes (use them all) and another quarter of the cake mixture.

6. Lastly, add the remaining pears and top with the remaining cake mixture. Tap the tin to remove any air, then bake in the preheated oven for 40 minutes. Allow to cool before turning out of the tin.

Serves 12

Light & Luscious Apple Crumble

Here is Catherine Saxelby's light version of the traditional winter pudding - it contains a tasty breakfast cereal which has a lovely texture and a delicate cinnamon flavour. For dessert, serve with Creamy No Stick Custard (page 88), or, for a nourishing breakfast, serve with yoghurt.

6 large green cooking apples, peeled and sliced

¹/₄ cup water

¹/₄ cup sugar (optional)

1¹/₄ cups All Bran Soy 'n Fibre cereal or muesli

¹/₄ cup wholemeal self-raising flour

¹/₄ cup brown sugar

2 tablespoons margarine

2 tablespoons honey

1. To cook the apples, place them in a saucepan with the water, and if using, the sugar. Cover and bring the mixture to the boil. Reduce the heat and cook the apples gently until they are soft, 15–20 minutes, then transfer them to an ovenproof dish.

2. To make the crumble topping, combine the cereal (or muesli) with the flour and sugar. Place the margarine and the honey in a small saucepan and heat gently until the margarine melts, then combine with the dry ingredients.

3. Sprinkle the crumble topping evenly over the apples and bake in a preheated oven at 200°C until golden brown, about 20 minutes.

Serves 4

ON OCCASION!

Serve with a scoop of vanilla ice cream dusted with cinnamon.

Apricot & Orange Purée (opposite)

Apricot & Orange Purée

This lovely purée is great for topping cakes and for serving as a dip with fresh fruit. For a special fruity dessert, layer it with plain yoghurt in attractive glasses.

1 cup dried apricots

3/4 cup orange juice

2 tablespoons honey

1. Put all the ingredients into a saucepan and bring the mixture to the boil. Reduce the heat, cover and cook over a low to medium heat until the apricots are tender, 10–15 minutes.

2. Blend the apricots with the cooking liquid until smooth.

Serves 4

Apricot Yoghurt Cream

This light fruity cream is much lower in fat than pure cream, but is just as good served with cakes, strudels and slices.

500 g thick plain skim-milk yoghurt

4 tablespoons Apricot & Orange Purée (this page)

Put the yoghurt into a mixing bowl and gradually stir in the Apricot & Orange Purée. For a cream with a pastel hue, combine the ingredients thoroughly. For a pale-coloured cream with streaks and swirls, stir the purée through but do not combine thoroughly.

Serves 4

Apple & Pear Pastries

A high-fat food, pastry is best eaten in small amounts, such as in this recipe. The crisp almond wafers make great partners for the cinnamon and orange-flavoured apples and pears. Serve with thick skim-milk yoghurt.

1 sheet frozen shortcrust pastry, thawed

1 egg, beaten

2–3 tablespoons flaked almonds

1–2 tablespoons castor sugar

2 medium-sized apples, peeled, cored and thickly sliced

2 medium-sized firm pears, peeled, cored and thickly sliced

1/2 cup water

3 tablespoons castor sugar (extra)

1/2 teaspoon cinnamon

1/2 cup freshly squeezed orange juice

1. Preheat the oven to 190°C.

2. Invert the pastry onto a baking tray and peel off the plastic film. Cut the pastry into four squares, then cut in half again on the diagonal to make triangles. Brush each triangle with the egg (take care not to brush the egg over the edges of the pastry) and sprinkle with the almonds and sugar.

3. Bake in the preheated oven until golden brown, 5–8 minutes. Rest for 2 minutes, then transfer the pastry wafers onto a cooling rack.

4. Place the apples, pears and water in a saucepan. Cover and bring to the boil over a medium heat, then reduce the heat and cook over a low to medium heat until the fruit is tender but firm and the water almost evaporated, 10–15 minutes. Stir in the sugar, cinnamon and orange juice and return the mixture to the boil. Remove from the stove and set aside to cool.

5. Spoon the fruit onto 4 serving plates. Arrange 2 pastry triangles on either side of the fruit and serve at once.

Serves 4

ON OCCASION!

Serve with a scoop of quality vanilla ice-cream.

Mango & Macadamia Whirl

Give this 'whirl' a burl — it makes a refreshing yet filling snack or breakfast when you are on the go! The nuts add a creamy richness.

1 mango, peeled and sliced

6 macadamias

2–3 teaspoons honey

1/4 teaspoon ground cinnamon

3 cups icy-cold low-fat milk

Blend all the ingredients until smooth and creamy and drink at once to ensure the best flavour and texture.

Serves 2

tip *In the cooler months, replace the mango with 1 large ripe banana or 1 cup peaches or apricots canned in their own juice.*

Berry Banana Smoothie

The banana in this delicious smoothie provides a thick and creamy texture and the strawberries add a refreshing tang.

1 ripe banana

1 cup strawberries, tops removed

2 teaspoons honey

3 cups icy-cold low-fat milk

1–2 tablespoons skim-milk powder

Blend all the ingredients together until smooth and creamy and drink at once to ensure the best flavour and texture.

Serves 2

tip *Adding skim-milk powder to smoothies and milk shakes creates a foamy top whilst boosting your calcium intake.*

This page: *Vanilla Iced Coffee on the Rocks* (page 92)
Opposite: *Ricotta & Chicken Balls with Apricot & Coriander* (page 80)
and *Roasted Red Capsicum Sauce* (page 35)

eat!
enjoy!

Dairy
Soy
&

These days a wide variety of dairy foods is right at our fingertips. Cute-looking

bocconcini 'cherries', chewy mozzarella, creamy ricotta, herb-infused

cottage cheese, crumbly feta and flavour-packed parmesan are all featured here.

Yoghurt travels right across the menu and soy foods such as

calcium-enriched soy drinks and tofu also come to the party.

Tasty Tofu Dip

This dip is very similar to hummus dip, but it has a lighter, smoother texture. It doubles as a creamy dressing to spoon on top of mixed salad greens. Remember to use tofu that has been prepared using calcium sulphate if you are especially looking to boost your calcium intake (check the ingredients label).

125 g tofu, drained

2 teaspoons lemon juice

2 tablespoons tahini paste

2–3 garlic cloves

2 tablespoons plain skim-milk yoghurt

1/2 teaspoon ground cumin

2 teaspoons salt-reduced soy sauce

1 teaspoon balsamic vinegar

1/4 teaspoon Tabasco sauce

1/4 teaspoon ground sweet paprika

1. Combine all the ingredients except for the paprika and blend until thoroughly combined and velvety smooth.

2. Transfer the dip to a serving bowl, cover and refrigerate until required. Just before serving, dust with the paprika.

Serves 4

Creamy Asparagus Soup

Soups are a great way to incorporate more calcium into your meals. Long gone are the rich thick soups based on a butter and flour thickening (roux). Simple vegetable soups like this one can still be rich and thick, by blending the vegetables with plenty of milk or calcium-enriched soy drink.

2–3 teaspoons olive oil

1 large onion, chopped

2 bunches (400 g) asparagus, trimmed and sliced

2–3 garlic cloves, chopped

1 cup vegetable stock

3 cups low-fat milk or calcium-enriched soy drink

pepper

sweet paprika or freshly ground nutmeg (garnish)

1. Heat the oil in a large saucepan and stir-fry the onion over a high heat for 1 minute. Reduce the heat to low, cover and cook for 10 minutes, stirring occasionally.

2. Add the asparagus and garlic, stirring to mix through. Cover and continue to cook over a low heat for 5 minutes. Stir through the vegetable stock, then cover and cook over a medium heat for 5 minutes.

3. Remove from the heat and blend the soup until smooth with the milk. Reheat gently, then season to taste with the pepper, dust with the paprika (or nutmeg) and serve at once.

Serves 4–6

tip *For the best flavour, buy nutmeg whole and grate on a fine grater as needed. Whole nutmeg is available from the spice section of supermarkets, Asian grocery stores and delicatessens.*

Gnocchi with Pumpkin & Broccoli (opposite)

Gnocchi with Pumpkin & Broccoli

*This recipe is an example of achieving a rich pasta sauce
without dolloping on the butter or cream. Evaporated
low-fat milk is all that is needed to create this 'creamy' dish
which is beautifully offset by the steamed greens.*

1 tablespoon olive oil

1 onion, chopped

1 tablespoon sliced green
chillies, seeds removed

2 garlic cloves, crushed

600 g pumpkin, peeled, seeds
removed, cut into 1 cm cubes

1 x 375 ml can evaporated
low-fat milk

1/2 bunch spring onions, sliced,
green tops included

500–750 g fresh gnocchi
(depending on preferred
serving sizes)

250 g broccoli, trimmed, cut
into florets

1 bunch baby bok choy,
trimmed and cut in half
lengthways

cracked black pepper

1. Heat the oil in a large saucepan and stir-fry
the onion, chillies and garlic over a high heat for
2 minutes. Add the pumpkin, then reduce the
heat. Cover and cook, stirring occasionally, until
the pumpkin is tender, about 15 minutes.

2. Add the milk and half the spring onions to the
pan. Bring the sauce to the boil, stirring, then
reduce the heat, cover and cook over a medium
heat for 10 minutes, stirring occasionally.

3. Meanwhile, bring a large pan of water to the
boil and cook the gnocchi until just tender and
cooked through, about 5 minutes. (The gnocchi
is cooked not long after it rises to the surface of
the cooking water. Take care not to overcook it or
it will disintegrate.) Drain.

4. While the gnocchi is cooking, steam the bok
choy and broccoli until just tender and still a
vibrant green colour, about 5 minutes. Arrange
on serving plates.

5. Drain the gnocchi and toss with the sauce.
Arrange the gnocchi on the bok choy and
broccoli and scatter with the remaining spring
onions. Dust with the pepper and serve at once.

Serves 4

Kumera, Corn & Pasta Soup

*Kumera is an orange-coloured sweet potato that adds colour
and flavour to many dishes. This sweet and spicy soup makes
a lovely light meal served with warm focaccia or crusty rolls.
The rich texture of this soup comes from the kumera, which
cooks down to a mash, and the milk.*

1 tablespoon olive oil

1 onion, chopped

1 large kumera, peeled and
chopped

1 cup fresh, frozen or drained
canned corn kernels

1 cup fresh or frozen peas

2–3 garlic cloves, crushed

2–3 teaspoons sweet chilli
sauce

1 cup vegetable stock

3 cups low-fat milk

3 cups cooked pasta

cracked black pepper

1. Heat the oil in a large saucepan and stir-fry the
onion over a medium to high heat for 1 minute.
Stir in the kumera, corn and peas, then cover
and cook over a low to medium heat, stirring
occasionally until the kumera breaks down, about
10 minutes.

2. Add the garlic, chilli sauce and stock, then
bring the soup to the boil over a medium heat,
stirring constantly.

3. Stir in the milk and pasta and reheat gently,
stirring occasionally. Serve piping hot, dusted with
the pepper.

Serves 4–6

tip *Bow-tie pasta is especially suitable for
this recipe. It looks great and is easy to
eat. However, any type of short pasta will do.*

Golden Vegetable Rolls with Ricotta

There's no need to cut out high-fat/high-calcium cheeses such as parmesan. Instead, cut down on the amount used and balance it with low-fat cheeses such as ricotta, as in this recipe.

1/4 teaspoon olive oil

1 carrot, peeled and coarsely grated

8 spring onions, chopped, green tops included

250 g baby spinach or rocket leaves, well rinsed

1 garlic clove, crushed

250 g ricotta

4 tablespoons grated or shredded parmesan

1 egg, separated

a pinch each of pepper and nutmeg

8 large sheets filo pastry

2 tablespoons olive oil

2 tablespoons sesame seeds

1. Preheat the oven to 200°C. Brush the 1/4 teaspoon oil over a baking tray.

2. Heat 1 tablespoon water in a large saucepan and add the carrots, spring onions, spinach and garlic. Cover and cook over a medium heat for 5 minutes, stirring occasionally. Remove from the heat and set aside to cool.

3. Mix the ricotta, parmesan and egg white in a bowl, then combine with the vegetable mixture, pepper and nutmeg.

4. Work with 4 sheets of pastry at a time. Spread out 2 sheets of pastry on the bench and brush lightly with oil. Top with another two sheets of pastry and brush with oil.

5. Arrange half of the vegetable mixture in a row along the edge of the pastry closest to you, extending it right to the edges. Roll the pastry up firmly to form a long roll. Using a sharp knife, cut the roll into 3 or 6 slices. Repeat with the remaining pastry, oil and filling.

6. Arrange the rolls, seam side down, on the prepared baking tray. Brush with the reserved egg yolk and sprinkle with the sesame seeds.

7. Bake in the preheated oven until the filling is firm and the pastry is golden brown, 12–15 minutes.

Makes 6 large rolls or 12 small rolls

Tofu Vegetable Skewers (opposite)

Tofu Vegetable Skewers

A simple dish that can be varied according to the pesto you are in the mood for. They are just as good served on top of freshly cooked rice as in this recipe, or slipped off the skewers and wrapped in warmed tortillas. For a touch of colour and to boost the calcium content, serve with Roasted Capsicum & Yoghurt Sauce (page 84) or Yoghurt, Cucumber & Mint Sauce (page 84).

2 zucchini, cut into 0.5 cm slices

1 red capsicum, seeds removed, cut into 2 cm squares

12 baby button mushrooms

375 g firm tofu, cut into 2 cm cubes

4 tablespoons Pesto (page 36)

1 tablespoon salt-reduced soy sauce

1 teaspoon sesame oil

2 cups basmati rice

1–2 teaspoons turmeric

8 bamboo skewers, soaked in water for 30 minutes

1. Place the vegetables and tofu in a bowl and add the pesto, soy sauce and sesame oil. Toss all the ingredients together to coat evenly with the mixture.

2. Cover and set aside to marinate for at least 1 hour. Alternatively, leave in the refrigerator to marinate for 1 day.

3. Meanwhile, place the rice in a medium-sized saucepan with the turmeric. Stir in 3 cups water. Cover and bring to the boil, then reduce the heat and cook over a low heat until all the water has been absorbed, 12–15 minutes. Set aside.

4. Thread the vegetables and tofu alternately on the skewers and cook under a hot grill or on top of a hot barbecue until nicely browned, about 5 minutes on each side. (Brush the tofu and vegetables with any remaining marinade during cooking.)

Serves 4

Ricotta & Chicken Balls with Apricot & Coriander

These are very light in texture and are excellent for a light meal served with steamed or roasted vegetables. Or they can be made into balls the size of a walnut, and served as finger food with Yoghurt & Chilli Sauce (this page).

250 g lean minced chicken

250 g ricotta

1 egg, beaten

1/2 cup fresh breadcrumbs (see glossary)

1/2 cup dried apricots, chopped

finely grated zest of 1 lemon

1 tablespoon chopped mint

1 tablespoon chopped coriander

2 spring onions, chopped

2 teaspoons chilli sauce

coriander leaves (garnish)

1. Using a food processor, blend all the ingredients (except the garnish) until well combined.

2. Chill the mixture for 10–15 minutes in the refrigerator to allow the mixture to thicken, then form into small balls, the size of a plum.

3. Steam the chicken balls until the chicken is cooked, 5–8 minutes. (Take care not to overcook to ensure they are moist and succulent.)

4. Garnish with the coriander leaves and serve.

Serves 4 *(Pictured on page 71)*

Yoghurt & Chilli Sauce

1 cup plain skim-milk yoghurt

1 tablespoon sweet chilli sauce

1 tablespoon chopped mint

1 tablespoon chopped coriander

Combine all the ingredients and chill before serving.

Serves 4

Mozzarella Pesto Pizzarets

These are quick and easy, and make a great snack. They also make a delicious main meal with a bowl of steaming hot soup brimming with vegetables, such as Chilli Pumpkin Soup with Chick Peas (page 29).

4 tablespoons Semi-dried Tomato Pesto (page 36)

1 packet English-style muffins, split in half

4 large cap mushrooms, sliced

125 g pre-shredded low-fat mozzarella

1 capsicum, seeds removed, sliced

2 teaspoons dried basil

cracked black pepper

1. Preheat the oven to 200°C .

2. Spread the pesto evenly on the muffin halves. Arrange the mushrooms, mozzarella and capsicum on top, then sprinkle with the basil and pepper.

3. Bake in the preheated oven until lightly browned, about 20 minutes.

Makes 12

tip *Pre-shredded low-fat mozzarella cheese is available at larger supermarkets. Stir it through risotto and pilafs just before serving to give the dish that lovely 'stringy' texture typical of melted mozzarella. This is another delicious way to boost your calcium intake!*

Bocconcini & Roasted Tomato Salad (opposite)

Bocconcini & Roasted tomato Salad

Tender and flavoursome, this special salad only takes minutes to prepare. It is best prepared and served at room temperature to bring out the best of the flavours.

8 Roma tomatoes, cut in half lengthways

2 cups rocket or baby spinach leaves

12 bocconcini 'cherries', cut in half

1 tablespoon extra virgin olive oil

1 tablespoon balsamic vinegar

¹/₂ cup sliced basil leaves

60 g parmesan, shaved

cracked black pepper

1. Heat the griller and roast the tomatoes, cut side down, until the skins become blistered and charred. Set aside until cool enough to handle, then peel.

2. Place the rocket leaves on serving plates and arrange the roasted tomatoes on top. Tuck the bocconcini cherries in between the tomatoes.

3. Drizzle the salad first with the olive oil, then the vinegar. Scatter with the basil and parmesan, dust with the pepper and serve at once.

Serves 4

tip *Bocconcini cheese is a fresh stretched curd cheese formed into little domes referred to as 'cherries'. The cherries are sold immersed in a mild brine solution. Bocconcini has a delicate flavour and provides an interesting texture rather similar to al dente pasta. It is used to carry other flavours such as fresh herbs and olive oil in salads. When heated, as on top of pizzas, it melts into appetising creamy-coloured pools.*

Yummy Yoghurt Sauces

Yoghurt is an excellent source of calcium, so be sure to try these light and tasty sauces with a variety of dishes. For thicker sauces, try using Greek-style Yoghurt (page 88). For another delicious yoghurt sauce, see Yoghurt & Chilli Sauce (page 80).

Roasted Capsicum & Yoghurt Sauce

1 red capsicum, roasted (page 35)

1 cup plain skim-milk yoghurt

1–2 garlic cloves, crushed

a few drops of Tabasco sauce

Blend the capsicum until smooth, then transfer to a bowl and stir through the yoghurt, garlic and Tabasco.

Serves 4

Yoghurt, Cucumber & Mint Sauce

1 cup plain skim-milk yoghurt

2 tablespoons finely chopped mint

1 garlic clove, crushed

1 tablespoon sweet chilli sauce

pepper

1 Lebanese cucumber, peeled and finely diced

Mix all ingredients together, cover and chill before serving.

Serves 4

Catherine Saxelby's
Baked Ricotta Cheesecake

Catherine Saxelby is a nutritionist and accredited dietitian who is well known for her no-nonsense approach to the modern-day dilemma of how to eat healthy food within our fast food lifestyle. Her quest is to help busy people with little time to cook to prepare meals that are nutritious yet quick and easy to put together. Catherine is the author of *Nutrition for Life* and the *Busy Body Cookbook*, and offers nutrition advice on her website www.foodwatch.com.au

This recipe creates a light cheesecake which is a perfect summer dessert with fresh fruit. The filo provides a paper-thin outer shell instead of the usual (high fat) pastry or biscuit crumb crust and, as a bonus, facilitates easier cutting. For a delicious stunning dessert, serve with Maple Berry Sauce (page 57).

3 sheets filo pastry

oil spray

4 eggs

1/2 cup castor sugar

750 g ricotta

1 tablespoon vanilla essence

1 tablespoon flour

grated zest of 1 orange

2 tablespoons mixed peel (optional)

1. Preheat the oven to 160°C. Line an ungreased 20 cm springform pan with the filo, spraying each sheet of pastry lightly with the oil. With a pair of kitchen scissors, trim away any excess pastry so that it is level with the top of the tin.

2. Beat the eggs until light and fluffy, then add the sugar and mix well.

3. In a separate bowl, beat the ricotta until smooth, then combine with the vanilla, flour, zest and peel (if using) and the egg mixture. Pour the mixture into the lined pan and bake in the preheated oven until the centre of the filling is firm, 50–60 minutes.

4. Allow to cool. Chill before cutting into wedges.

Serves 10

Lemony Custard Cake (opposite) with *Poached Plums* (page 56)

Lemony Custard Cake

This cake is just made to be served with a 'saucy' accompaniment like the poached plums in this recipe, or Maple Berry Sauce (page 57).

¼ teaspoon soft margarine

½ cup hazelnut meal

⅔ cup wholemeal self-raising flour

finely grated zest of ½ lemon

3 tablespoons honey

2 tablespoons soft margarine

1 egg, beaten lightly

⅓ cup plain skim-milk yoghurt or milk

LEMONY CUSTARD

5 tablespoons custard powder

2 tablespoons sugar

2½ cups low-fat milk

3 tablespoons skim-milk powder

finely grated zest of ½ lemon

double quantity Poached Plums (page 56)

1. Preheat the oven to 200°C. Brush the inside of a 20 cm cake tin (preferably springform) with the ¼ teaspoon of the margarine.

2. To make the base, combine the hazelnut meal, flour and lemon zest. In a separate bowl, combine the honey, margarine, egg and yoghurt. Add to the dry ingredients, mixing thoroughly. Spread the mixture out in an even layer in the prepared tin. Bake in the preheated oven until golden, about 20 minutes.

3. To make the custard in the microwave oven, see the method for Creamy No Stick Custard (page 88), replacing the vanilla with the lemon zest.

4. To make the custard on top of the stove, use a wooden spoon to blend the custard powder to a smooth paste with ¼ cup of the milk in a heatproof bowl. Bring the remaining milk to simmering point in a saucepan over a medium to high heat. Stir the hot milk through the custard powder paste, then return the mixture to the saucepan. Stirring occasionally with the wooden spoon, bring the mixture to the boil, then simmer for 1–2 minutes. Stir in the milk powder and lemon zest.

5. Spread the hot custard in an even layer on top of the prepared base and set aside to cool and chill thoroughly. To serve, arrange slices of the cake on individual plates with 1 or 2 of the Poached Plums, spooning a little of the cooking liquid over. Serve at once.

Serves 8–10

Creamy No Stick Custard

A quick and easy custard that even the kids can make. Cooking custard in a microwave oven involves a less direct heat compared to the on-top-of-the-stove method, therefore the custard does not stick to the bowl it is cooked in. You can enjoy this custard without having to worry about the custard-encrusted saucepan lurking in the sink!

2 tablespoons custard powder

2 tablespoons skim-milk powder

1 tablespoon sugar

2 cups low-fat milk

a few drops vanilla extract

1. Place the custard powder, skim milk powder and sugar in a microwave ovenproof bowl. Using a wooden spoon, mix to a smooth paste with 1/4 cup of the milk, then stir through the remaining milk.

2. Cook in a microwave oven on High for 6 minutes, removing the custard from the oven every 2 minutes to stir thoroughly. Stir through the vanilla extract and serve hot or cold.

Serves 4

Greek-Style Yoghurt

This lovely thick yoghurt is great for making dips, using in place of sour cream and dolloping on to fresh, stewed and baked fruits.

1.5 litres plain skim-milk yoghurt

Line a sieve with a clean piece of cheesecloth or a new Chux Supa Wipe. Rest the sieve over a bowl. Pour the yoghurt into the cloth, then fold the ends of the cloth over the yoghurt. Set aside in the refrigerator for 4 hours, then transfer the thick yoghurt to a fresh container.

Makes about 4 cups

Lassies

*A mixture of icy-cold fruit juice and plain yoghurt, lassies are
a great pick-me-up on a hot day. For people on the move,
they are great to have when you are in too much of a hurry for
a sit-down breakfast. (But have a sandwich or an uniced fruit
bun for morning tea to make sure you have plenty of energy
to carry you through to lunchtime!)*

Great Grape Lassi

**3 cups icy-cold dark grape
juice (no added sugar)**

**2 cups plain skim-milk
yoghurt**

Blend the grape juice with the yoghurt until
smooth and creamy. Pour into 2 long glasses and
serve at once.

Serves 2

Amazing Apricot Lassi

*This lassi has a luscious sweet and spicy flavour,
and a creamy golden hue.*

3 cups icy-cold apricot nectar

**2 cups plain skim-milk
yoghurt**

**¼ teaspoon ground
cinnamon**

Blend all the ingredients until smooth and creamy.
Pour into 2 long glasses and serve at once.

Serves 2

Mini Mango Freezecakes (opposite) with *Creamy Coulis* (opposite)

Mini Mango Freezecakes

These stunning little frozen cheesecakes are surprisingly simple to prepare.

½ teaspoon mild-flavoured oil

250 g reduced-fat cream cheese e.g Light Philly cheese

250 g plain skim-milk yoghurt

4 tablespoons mild-flavoured honey

1 teaspoon vanilla extract

2 mangoes, peeled and chopped

12 granita or shredded wheatmeal biscuits

fresh fruit and mint sprigs (garnish)

1. Brush the muffin tray with the oil.

2. Blend the cream cheese, yoghurt, honey, vanilla and half the mangoes until smooth. Transfer the mixture to a mixing bowl and stir in the remaining mangoes.

3. Spoon the mixture into the muffin tray, then top each one with a biscuit.

4. Put the muffin tray in the freezer and allow at least 3 hours for the cakes to freeze. Remove from the freezer 5–10 minutes before required.

5. Using a knife, loosen the cheesecakes around the edges. Carefully turn out the number of freezecakes you need onto serving plates, returning any remaining cakes to the freezer. Decorate with fresh fruit and mint sprigs and serve at once.

Makes 12

Creamy Coulis

The yoghurt in this fruity sauce produces the creamy texture.

1 cup chopped mango, strawberries or loganberries

1 tablespoon lemon juice

2–3 teaspoons castor sugar

1 cup plain skim-milk yoghurt

1. Blend the fruit with the lemon juice and sugar.

2. Transfer the purée to a bowl and fold in the yoghurt until well combined. If not using at once, store in the refrigerator.

Serves 4

Vanilla Iced Coffee on the Rocks

This light and lovely iced coffee is a welcome alternative to rich, creamy iced coffee smothered in whipped cream. It is perfect for anyone looking for delicious low-fat ways to include more calcium in their diets.

8 Vanilla Ice Blocks (this page)

½ cup strong coffee, chilled

2 cups chilled low-fat milk

1. Put 4 milk ice blocks into each of 2 long glasses.

2. Divide the coffee between the 2 glasses, add the milk and enjoy!

Serves 2 *(pictured on Page 70)*

ON OCCASION!

Top with a scoop of vanilla ice-cream and sprinkle with shaved chocolate. Serve as a delicious finale to a special summer meal – better than a rich dessert, and more refreshing too!

Vanilla Ice Blocks

These are great to add to chilled milk drinks and to cool kids down on hot days.

1½ cups low-fat milk

2 teaspoons vanilla extract

2–3 teaspoons maple syrup (optional)

1. In a jug, combine the milk, vanilla and, if using, the maple syrup.

2. Pour into ice-block trays and freeze for at least 2 hours.

ON OCCASION!

Replace the vanilla with liqueur such as Kahlua or crème de cacao.

Milk & Honey Soother

There's something about hot milk and honey that makes the eyelids heavy and the whole body relax . . . and besides, these types of drinks are nutritious as well as delicious.

2¹/₂ cups low-fat milk

2 teaspoons honey

3 teaspoons coffee substitute (optional)

Place the milk and honey in a small saucepan and heat to just below boiling point, stirring to dissolve the honey. If using a coffee substitute, whisk it through the milk as it is heating. Pour the drink into 2 coffee mugs and serve at once.

Serves 2

Spiced tea with Milk & Honey

This brew makes a warming drink on a cold day or a soothing drink after a long day at any time of the year. In fact, it is a lovely drink to offer a loved one when a little nurturing is needed . . .

3 teaspoons black tea leaves or 3 teapot tea bags

2 cm piece fresh ginger, sliced

¹/₂ stick cinnamon

2–3 cardamom pods

1¹/₂ cups boiling water

2 cups low-fat milk

2 teaspoons honey

1. Heat a teapot by filling it with boiling water. Allow it to stand for a few minutes, then empty the teapot and add the tea leaves, ginger, cinnamon and cardamom. Top with the 1¹/₂ cups boiling water, cover and set aside for 5 minutes to allow the flavours to infuse.

2. Meanwhile, place the milk and honey in a small saucepan and heat to just below boiling point, stirring to dissolve the honey. Strain the tea through a fine strainer into 2 large cups or mugs, then using a teaspoon, stir in the hot milk and honey. Pour into 2 coffee mugs and serve immediately.

Serves 2

This page: *Chicken & Lemongrass on Parade* (page 100) with
Cucumber & Coriander Salad (Page 101); Opposite: *Thai Fish Cake* (page 99)

eat! enjoy!

Meat, Fish & chicken

Think low-fat and high-flavour and you've got the gist of this chapter!
Clever cooking methods, lively herbs and spices, tasty marinades and tangy

citrus juices are teamed up with an ever-increasing variety of lean meat,

fish and chicken to create stunning dishes with a minimum of fuss.

Spinach & Prawn Soup

This is a light yet comforting soup. Serve it with a crusty breadstick to mop up every last flavoursome drop.

350 g green (raw) prawns

1 tablespoon peanut oil

1 onion, chopped

2 garlic cloves, chopped

1 small bunch spinach, washed well and dried

1/2 teaspoon turmeric

2 cups fish stock or prawn stock (see tip)

11/2 teaspoons fish sauce

1/2 cup light coconut milk or evaporated low-fat milk

1 small chilli, seeds removed, chopped

1. Wash, shell and devein the prawns. Set aside the prawn heads and shells to make the stock (see tip). Retain 4 prawns to decorate the finished soup, then roughly chop the remaining prawns and set aside.

2. Heat the oil in a saucepan and stir-fry the garlic and onion over a medium heat until soft.

3. Cut the stalks off the spinach and chop. Set the leaves aside. Add the chopped stalks to the pan with the turmeric, stock and fish sauce. Simmer for 5–10 minutes, then add the spinach leaves and cook for 2 minutes.

4. Blend the soup, coconut milk and the chilli until smooth. Pour the soup into a saucepan and add the chopped prawns. Heat over a low–medium heat until the prawns are just cooked, 2–3 minutes.

5. Ladle the soup into bowls and top each serve with a whole cooked prawn.

Serves 4 *(Pictured on page 31)*

tip *TO MAKE PRAWN STOCK: Heat 1 tablespoon oil in a frying pan and cook the prawn shells and heads over a high heat until they become pink. Stir in 4 cups of water and bring the mixture to the boil. Reduce the heat and simmer until the mixture has reduced by half, 20–30 minutes. Strain the stock through a sieve and if not using at once, store in an airtight container in the refrigerator.*

Catch-of-the-Day Fish Soup

Serve with fresh bread and a bowl of Zesty Herb Sprinkle (this page).

1 tablespoon olive oil

1 large leek, finely sliced

1 onion, finely sliced

2 garlic cloves, finely chopped

3 cm piece lemongrass

2 strips orange zest

1/2 teaspoon fennel seeds

1/2 teaspoon saffron threads, soaked in 1/4 cup warm water

1 x 425 g can crushed tomatoes

11/2 cups dry white wine

cracked black pepper

500 g fish fillets, cut into bite-sized chunks

500 g fresh mussels, beards removed, scrubbed

1. Heat the oil in a deep saucepan, and stir-fry the leek and onion over medium heat until soft but not coloured, 3–4 minutes.

2. Add the garlic, lemongrass, orange zest, fennel seeds and saffron mixture and cook for 1–2 minutes. Stir in the tomatoes, wine and pepper. Cover and simmer for 15 minutes.

3. Remove the lemongrass and orange zest and add the fish and mussels. Cover and cook until the mussel shells have opened, about 5 minutes.

Serves 4 *(Pictured on page 31)*

tips *Select the fish according to what is best at the market, but choose firm-fleshed fish such as flathead and trevally as they hold their shape better.*

The mussels can be replaced with a mixture of calamari rings and prawns.

Zesty Herb Sprinkle

A lovely mix to sprinkle on top of soups and salads.

1/2 cup finely chopped parsley

2 garlic cloves, finely chopped

finely grated zest of 1 lemon

Combine all the ingredients. If not using at once, store in a jar in the refrigerator.

Dill & Ginger Marinated Fillets

Choose any white fish fillet you like for this quick and easy dish.
Serve with fluffy mashed potatoes and a colourful salad.

2 tablespoons olive oil

4 tablespoons lemon juice

2 tablespoons teriyaki sauce

1 garlic clove, crushed

1 teaspoon finely chopped
ginger

2 teaspoons sweet chilli sauce

2 tablespoons dill,
finely chopped

4 x 130 g fish fillets such as
rockling, snapper or flathead

1. Combine all the ingredients and spread the mixture evenly over the fish fillets. Cover and set aside in the refrigerator to marinate for 15–30 minutes.

2. To cook in the oven, wrap the fish individually in foil and bake in an oven preheated to 180°C until the fish is creamy white and moist in the thickest part, 10–12 minutes. Serve immediately.

3. To cook in a microwave oven, place the fish in a microwave-proof dish, cover with plastic film and cook on High for 4–5 minutes, depending on the thickness of the fish used. (Remember to allow for the carry-over cooking time after the fish is removed from the microwave oven – it's best to undercook the fish slightly and then allow it to stand, covered, for a couple of minutes in a warm place before serving).

Serves 4

ON Occasion!

Serve with chunky chips cooked until golden brown and crispy – the ultimate fish and chips!

thai Fish Cakes

4 medium-sized flathead fillets

1 egg, beaten

1 teaspoon chopped chillies

2 tablespoons chopped
coriander

2 tablespoons shredded coconut

1/2 teaspoon five-spice powder

1 kaffir lime leaf, sliced thinly

1 teaspoon fish sauce

2 spring onions, chopped

1/4 cup sesame seeds (optional)

1 tablespoon canola oil

1 quantity Lime Dressed Salad
(this page)

1. Using a food processor or blender, process the
fish, egg, chilli and coriander until smooth,
about 1 minute. Transfer the mixture to a bowl
and combine with the coconut, seasonings and
spring onions. If you have time, refrigerate the
fish mixture for 15 minutes before forming into
cakes and you will find the mixture firmer and
easier to handle.

2. Form the mixture into small cakes and, if
using, roll them in the sesame seeds.

3. Heat 2 teaspoons of the oil in a non-stick
frying pan and cook half the fish cakes until
golden brown, 2–3 minutes on each side.
Add the remaining oil to the pan and cook the
rest of the fish cakes.

4. Arrange the salad on serving plates and top
with the fish cakes.

Serves 4 *(Pictured on page 95)*

Lime Dressed Salad

200 g mixed lettuce leaves

2 tablespoons finely sliced mint

2 tablespoons chopped
coriander

LIME DRESSING

3 tablespoons lime juice

6 teaspoons peanut oil

1 teaspoon palm sugar or
brown sugar

1. Toss the lettuce with the mint and coriander.

2. Combine the dressing ingredients and, just
before serving, toss with the greens.

Serves 4

tip *Store fresh herbs wrapped in slightly
damp newspaper in a plastic bag in the
refrigerator and they will keep for over a week.*

Chicken & Lemongrass on Parade

Succulent pieces of spicy chicken lined up on lemongrass skewers pick up the fragrance of lemongrass as they cook. The Cucumber and Coriander Salad adds a fresh touch and completes the parade presentation.

1 teaspoon finely chopped red chilli

2 garlic cloves, chopped

2 teaspoons chopped ginger

2 teaspoons turmeric

1 teaspoon cumin

juice of 1 lime or lemon

4 chicken fillets, cut into 3 cm pieces

4 stalks lemongrass, cut into lengths for skewers (see tip)

1 tablespoon peanut oil

1 quantity Cucumber & Coriander Salad (opposite)

1. Combine the chilli, garlic and ginger with the turmeric, cumin and lime juice in a bowl. Add the chicken pieces and mix well. Cover and set aside in the refrigerator for at least 1 hour to allow the flavours to develop.

2. Using the point of a small sharp knife, make a small slit in each chicken piece and thread the chicken onto the lemongrass 'skewers', leaving a little space in between to show off the lovely green hue of the lemongrass.

3. Heat a barbecue or non-stick frying pan, brush with a little of the oil and cook the chicken skewers over a medium heat until the chicken is creamy white and moist inside, 5–7 minutes.

4. Arrange the skewers on serving plates with the Cucumber & Coriander Salad alongside.

Serves 4 *(Pictured on page 94)*

tips *TO MAKE LEMONGRASS 'SKEWERS': Strip off the outside leaves and cut the stalks into lengths of about 15 cm, or, for small neat skewers, cut the stalks in half, retaining the base to use in other dishes (wrap the unused base in plastic film and store in the refrigerator).*

You can replace the lemongrass with bamboo skewers, but be sure to presoak them in water for 30 minutes to prevent them from burning.

Cucumber & Coriander Salad

A perfect partner for Chicken & Lemongrass on Parade (opposite). This tangy light salad complements meat, fish and poultry dishes beautifully. To make into a main meal salad, see tip below.

1 continental cucumber or 3 Lebanese cucumbers, finely sliced

1 teaspoon chopped red chilli, seeds removed

juice of 1 lime or lemon

1 tablespoon palm sugar or brown sugar

1 tablespoon white wine vinegar

2 tablespoons chopped coriander

Place the cucumber in a serving bowl. Combine the chilli, lime juice, sugar and vinegar and pour over the cucumber. Scatter with the coriander and, if possible, chill before serving.

Serves 4 *(Pictured on page 94)*

tip *To make a delicious chicken salad, steam 2 chicken fillets until cooked through, about 10 minutes. (Add your choice of fresh or dried herbs to the water in the steamer, for herb scented chicken). Allow the chicken to cool, then slice and toss with 1 quantity Cucumber & Coriander Salad and serve on a bed of rocket leaves or steamed baby bok choy.*

Honey & Rosemary Lamb Fillets

Simply add lightly steamed vegetables for a quick and delicious meal.

500 g lamb fillets, trimmed

1 tablespoon honey

2 tablespoons lemon juice

2 tablespoons olive oil

1 garlic clove, crushed

1 tablespoon chopped rosemary

pepper

1 quantity Roasted Garlic Potato Mash (this page)

1. Remove the silver membrane from the fillets and place the fillets in a shallow dish.

2. Combine all other ingredients and pour over fillets, turning to coat them well. Cover and refrigerate for at least 1 hour or until ready to cook.

3. Cook the fillets on a hot barbecue, or in a very hot pan until they are a rich brown on all sides but still pale pink and juicy on the inside.

Serves 4

tip *Lamb fillets are lean, tender and very low in fat. Allow the meat to soak up the flavour of the marinade – overnight if possible.*

Roasted Garlic Potato Mash

4 medium-sized potatoes, peeled and halved

1/4 cup milk

pepper

1 tablespoon olive oil

5 cloves roasted garlic (page 155)

1 tablespoon finely chopped parsley

1. Place the potatoes in a saucepan and barely cover with cold water. Cover the pan and bring to the boil. Reduce the heat and cook, covered, until tender, about 15 minutes. Drain the water, and shake the pan over the heat to dry the potatoes. Mash the potatoes.

2. Heat the milk, then whisk into the potatoes. Season with pepper, then stir in the olive oil, garlic and parsley. Serve piping hot.

Serves 4

Pesto Lamb with Mediterranean Vegetables

Once the tasty vegies are bubbling in the pan, the lamb can be popped under a grill and cooked at the same time. The pesto adds pizzazz to grilled lamb. This flavour-packed dish is wonderful served with Creamy Polenta (page 136) which can be whipped up while the lamb is cooking.

1 tablespoon olive oil

1 onion, chopped

1 red capsicum, seeds removed, diced

2 zucchini, diced

1 small eggplant, diced

1 x 425 g can Tomatoes & Herbs

¼ cup white wine (optional)

400 g trim lamb fillets

2 tablespoons Sweet Basil Pesto or Semi-Dried Tomato Pesto (page 36)

a few drops of Tabasco sauce

1. Preheat the griller.

2. Heat the oil in a frying pan or a large saucepan and add the onion, capsicum, zucchini and eggplant. Stir-fry the mixture over a medium to high heat for 5 minutes, then stir in the Tomatoes & Herbs and, if using, the wine.

3. Reduce the heat to low or medium. Cook, uncovered, stirring occasionally, until the vegetables are tender, about 15 minutes.

4. Meanwhile, cook the lamb under a medium heat until cooked on one side. Turn the lamb over and continue grilling for 3 minutes. Spread the pesto over the lamb and cook only until heated through.

5. Season the vegetable mixture with the Tabasco and divide it between 4 serving plates. Arrange the lamb alongside and serve at once.

Serves 4

 For a vegetarian equivalent, replace the trim lamb with sliced firm tofu or tempeh.

DURÉ-DARA'S
Grilled Chicken
with WASABI & HERBS

Duré-Dara, a trained social worker, musician and restaurateur, has had an enormous impact on what Melburnians eat. In July 1997 she concluded her co-proprietorship of *Stephanie's Restaurant* after a twenty-year association. She is now a partner in *Donovans* at St Kilda Beach and the *Nudel Bar* in Bourke Street, Melbourne. She is President of the Restaurant and Catering Association of Victoria and Convenor of the Victorian Women's Trust.

The vibrant green of the wasabi and herb mixture against the light golden brown of the grilled chicken makes this a stunning dish. Duré says, 'I like to serve my grilled chicken with green tea noodles and soused spinach, or with fingers of polenta and grilled vegetables. Suit yourself according to what you have in the refrigerator and pantry. That decision is an enjoyable part of food preparation. Eat well, with pleasure and a sense of enjoyment.'

1 teaspoon Dijon mustard

1 teaspoon olive oil

1 garlic clove, crushed

4 lean skinless chicken fillets

1 tablespoon chopped dill

1 tablespoon chopped coriander

1 tablespoon chopped chives

1 teaspoon wasabi paste

1 tablespoon olive oil

cracked black pepper

1. Preheat the griller.

2. Combine the mustard and 1 teaspoon olive oil in a cup. Brush half of the mixture over the chicken fillets and cook them under a low to medium heat for about 5 minutes.

3. Turn the chicken over, brush the other side with the mustard mixture and continue to cook until the chicken is cooked through and lightly browned, about 5 minutes.

4. Meanwhile, combine the dill, coriander, chives, wasabi paste, 1 tablespoon olive oil and pepper. When the chicken is cooked, top each serve with the wasabi and herb mixture.

Serves 4

Middle-Eastern Spiced Lamb Roll-ups

This recipe adds a spicy twist to ever popular roast lamb.

500 g trim lamb topside

1 teaspoon garam masala

1 teaspoon ground cumin

pepper

2–3 garlic cloves, chopped

2 teaspoons olive oil

2 tablespoons lemon juice

1/4 cup mint leaves, chopped

4 rounds pita bread or souvlaki bread

1 quantity Orange & Tandoori Yoghurt Dip (page 53) or Yoghurt, Cucumber & Mint Sauce (page 84)

1. Using a sharp knife, score the top of the meat in a deep diamond pattern. Rub the garam masala, cumin and pepper into all sides of the meat.

2. Combine the remaining ingredients together and spread the mixture evenly over the meat. Wrap the meat in foil and refrigerate until ready to cook. (Allow at least 1 hour or leave to marinate overnight to allow the flavours to penetrate the meat.)

3. Cook the meat in an oven preheated to 200°C or on a hot barbecue until medium to well done, 20–30 minutes. If cooking in the oven, remove the top of the foil for the last 10 minutes of the cooking time to allow the meat to brown.

4. Remove from the oven and allow the meat to rest for 10 minutes before slicing. Meanwhile, warm the pita bread (or souvlaki bread) in the oven. Arrange the meat on the bread and drizzle with your choice of dip or sauce. Roll up the bread and serve at once.

Serves 4

tip *To make these roll-ups more filling, add 2–3 tablespoonfuls of tabouli salad to each serve before rolling up. To make your own, see Terrific Tabouli Salad (page 19). Or buy prepared tabouli salad from larger supermarkets and delicatessens.*

Ian Parmenter's
Lamb Shank & tomato Ragout

Ian Parmenter is well known to television audiences through his highly acclaimed ABC TV show *Consuming Passions*, now in its eighth season. Ian's quest is to demonstrate that cooking should always be fun, and to try to coax people back in the kitchen, with an underlying nutritional message. Ian's latest book, *L Plates*, is published by JB Fairfax and is available at all ABC shops and centres, selected bookshops and newsagents.

Says Ian, 'Lamb shanks are another of those flavourful, cheaper meat cuts, which work really well in slow-simmered dishes. Ask your butcher to cut the shanks through the bone so they can be folded over.'

4 lamb shanks, trimmed

8 small garlic cloves, peeled

4 sprigs parsley

4 sprigs rosemary

2 tablespoons extra-virgin olive oil

1 cup red wine

1 medium-sized carrot, grated

1 stalk celery, finely chopped

1 leek, finely sliced

1 kg ripe tomatoes or 2 x 410 g cans tomatoes

500 g pasta of your choice, cooked

1. Fold over each lamb shank and tie up with string. Insert 2 garlic cloves and a sprig each of parsley and rosemary into the cracks of each lamb shank.

2. Heat the oil in a large deep pan and cook the shanks over a medium heat for about 5 minutes, turning them as they cook. Remove and set aside.

3. Splash the pan with the red wine and stir to deglaze the pan. Add the carrot, celery and leek and cook over a low heat for 5 minutes.

4. If using fresh tomatoes, peel them (page 112), and chop the flesh roughly.

5. Return the shanks to the pan and add the tomatoes. Cover tightly and simmer over a low heat until the meat falls off the bone, about 3 hours.

6. Remove the shanks from the sauce and discard the herbs, string and bones. Arrange the pasta on serving plates and top with the meat and sauce.

Serves 4

Thai Beef Salad

*Succulent thin strips of rare beef in a Thai-flavoured dressing
make this a perfect dish for a warm summer evening.
Serve this lovely salad with plenty of crusty bread.*

500 g rump steak, trimmed

pepper

200 g rocket or mixed lettuce leaves

2 Lebanese cucumbers, sliced thinly

1 punnet cherry tomatoes

2 tablespoons mint leaves, finely sliced

THAI-STYLE DRESSING

2 garlic cloves

1/4 cup coriander leaves

1–2 small red chillies, seeds removed and chopped

2 tablespoons lime or lemon juice

1 tablespoon fish sauce

1 tablespoon palm sugar or brown sugar

6 spring onions, sliced

1. Season the meat well with the pepper and seal in a non-stick pan over a high heat until well browned on both sides but rare inside. (Depending on the pan used, you may need to brush the pan surface lightly with oil to prevent the meat from sticking). Transfer the meat to a plate and allow it to rest for 4–5 minutes to let the meat fibres relax and help keep the juices in the meat.

2. Slice the meat thinly across the grain and place in a bowl. Add the rocket (or mixed lettuce leaves), cucumber, cherry tomatoes and mint.

3. To make the dressing, place the garlic, coriander, chillies, lime juice, fish sauce and spring onions in a food processor and process until well blended, about 1 minute.

4. Toss the beef and salad vegetables with the dressing and serve at once.

Serves 4

tip *Slice the meat across the grain to achieve the most tender eating quality. This is important when cutting raw meat and when carving roasts.*

Beef Keftas

Roasted walnuts, garlic and ginger season these lean beef keftas which are served with a refreshing fruit salsa. Serve with coleslaw salad or wrap the keftas with the salsa, and a heaped spoonful of Terrific Tabouli Salad (page 19) in warmed pita breads or mountain bread and serve as a light meal.

1/4 teaspoon canola oil

500 g lean minced beef

1/2 cup walnuts, roasted (this page) and chopped

2 cloves garlic, crushed

5 cm piece fresh ginger, peeled and finely chopped

1 egg, beaten

1 1/2 tablespoons teriyaki sauce

12 bamboo skewers, soaked in water for 30 minutes

1 tablespoon canola oil

2 tablespoons teriyaki sauce (extra)

1 quantity Pineapple Mint Salsa (page 55)

1. Preheat the oven to 200°C. Brush a large baking tray with the 1/4 teaspoon oil.

2. To make the keftas, thoroughly combine all the ingredients except for the 1 tablespoon canola oil, 2 tablespoons teriyaki sauce and Pineapple Mint Salsa. With wet hands, make 12 football-shaped keftas and thread each onto the skewers.

3. Combine the canola oil and teriyaki sauce. Brush the keftas with the mixture and arrange them on the prepared baking tray.

4. Bake in the preheated oven for 10–15 minutes, turning once and brushing with more of the oil and teriyaki mixture. Alternatively, cook under a hot griller for 8–10 minutes, brushing with the mixture 3–4 times during cooking.

5. Arrange the keftas on serving plates with the Pineapple Mint Salsa and your choice of accompaniments.

Serves 4

tip *TO ROAST NUTS AND SEEDS: Spread the nuts or seeds out on a baking tray and bake in a 190°C oven until a light golden brown, about 15 minutes. Alternatively, put them in a heavy-based frying pan (no oil is needed) and shake the pan over a medium heat until they are lightly browned, about 5 minutes.*

Gentle Coriander Beef Curry

This is the sort of dish that is better eaten the day after it is made. Serve with rice and chapattis or roti (available from larger supermarkets and Indian grocery stores) and for a special fruity touch, accompany with fresh or canned lychees.

1 tablespoon peanut oil

1 large onion, finely chopped

1 clove garlic, chopped

500 g blade bone or oyster blade steak, trimmed and cut into 3 cm cubes

2 teaspoons garam masala

3–4 fresh coriander roots, scraped and chopped

1 small red chilli, seeds removed and chopped

1 tablespoon tomato paste

1 medium-sized eggplant, trimmed and cut into cubes

2 cups beef stock

3 tablespoons plain skim-milk yoghurt

2 tablespoons chopped coriander leaves

1. Heat oil in a saucepan and cook the onion and garlic over a medium heat until soft but not brown. Add the meat and brown on all sides, then add the garam masala, coriander roots, chilli, tomato paste, eggplant and beef stock.

2. Cover and simmer for 45 minutes to 1 hour or until the meat is tender. (Remember to use a low heat to prevent the meat from becoming tough.)

3. Stir in the yoghurt and coriander and serve.

Serves 4

tip *Remember if you want to chill hot food quickly and safely, divide it into containers with no more than 8–10 cm depth and place in a refrigerator to cool.*

Honest to Goodness Beef Stew

This is almost a meal in one and only needs a green vegetable such as lightly cooked green beans for balance. There is no added fat in this dish but plenty of flavour!

500 g blade bone steak, trimmed and cut into 3 cm cubes

2 tablespoons plain flour

pepper

2 onions, finely chopped

1 stalk celery, sliced

2 cloves garlic, finely chopped

1/2 teaspoon fennel seeds

finely grated zest and sliced flesh of 2 oranges

1 tablespoon balsamic vinegar

1 cinnamon stick

1 cup red wine

1 cup water

1 large sweet potato, cut into chunks

1 cup cooked or canned beans, such as cannellini beans, drained

2 tablespoons chopped parsley (garnish)

1. Preheat the oven to 170°C. Toss the meat in the flour, season with the pepper and place in an ovenproof dish. Add the remaining ingredients except for the beans and parsley. Cover with a tight-fitting lid and cook in the preheated oven at until the meat is tender, about 2 hours.

2. Add the beans for the last 10 minutes of cooking. Sprinkle with parsley before serving.

Serves 4–6

 For a change, use lean boned lamb or pork instead of the beef.

A stew is usually cooked on top of the stove but if you cook it in the oven in a tightly covered casserole you will find the result is particularly moist and tender. One of the secrets is to use a casserole that is only just big enough to contain the ingredients – this allows for good flavour development and none of the juices will evaporate. Use a tight-fitting lid to cover or place a layer of foil before you put the lid on.

Mushroom Minute Steaks

Red wine, mushroom and mustard flavour these delicious pan-cooked minute steaks. This is a dish that must be enjoyed as soon as it is cooked so that the beef is tender and has no chance to toughen. Serve on a bed of Carrot Parsnip Mash (Page 46) or, Creamy Polenta (Page 136) with steamed seasonal greens on the side.

2 tablespoons canola oil

400 g silverside steak beef schnitzels, each cut into 3 pieces

300 g button mushrooms, sliced

1/2 cup dry red wine

1–2 teaspoons Dijon mustard

1/2 cup water

cracked black pepper

1 cup shredded spinach leaves or flat-leaf parsley leaves

1. Heat a large heavy-based frying pan, and add 1 tablespoon of the oil. Cook the beef in 2–3 batches over high heat for 1–2 minutes, turning once, then transfer to a plate to rest.

2. Heat the remaining oil in the frying pan. Add the mushrooms and stir over a high heat until the mushrooms soften slightly. Add the red wine and bring the sauce to the boil. Cook rapidly for about 1 minute to allow the alcohol to evaporate, and to deglaze the pan.

3. Stir in the mustard and water and return the sauce to the boil. Season with the pepper and stir in the spinach or parsley.

4. Return the beef and any juices to the pan and simmer for 1–2 minutes to heat through, then serve at once.

Serves 4

tips *Always use lean beef, but vary the cut by using thinly sliced strips of rump, sirloin, fillet or topside. Never keep turning the meat during cooking. When ready to turn, beads of moisture appear on the surface of the meat and the meat will release itself from the pan.*

Use tongs when turning meat – a fork can pierce the meat and allow the juices to escape.

Chilli avocado Steaks

Chargrilled sirloin steaks served on crisp lettuce leaves and warmed tortillas.

3 x 150–200 g lean sirloin steaks

1 tablespoon canola oil

1 large firm ripe avocado

1 tablespoon lemon juice

1/4 teaspoon dried red pepper flakes or 2 teaspoons chilli sauce to taste

4 tortillas

12 small to medium-sized cos lettuce leaves

1 quantity Onion & Tomato Salsa (this page)

1. Heat a heavy-based plain or ribbed pan over high heat. Brush the steaks with the oil, add to the pan and cook for 2–3 minutes on each side to seal, turning once only. Reduce the heat to medium or low and cook to your desired taste.

2. Mash the avocado in a bowl with the lemon juice and chilli flakes.

3. Heat the tortillas according to the directions on the packet. Fold each tortilla into four and put 1 tortilla onto each serving plate with 3 lettuce leaves. Top with a dollop of the avocado mixture.

4. Cut each steak into 4 portions and arrange 3 portions on top of each serving with a spoonful of the salsa.

Serves 4 *(Pictured on front cover and page 114)*

Onion & tomato Salsa

1 medium-sized red onion, finely diced

2 ripe tomatoes, peeled (see tip), seeded and flesh finely diced

1 teaspoon finely grated lemon zest

1 tablespoon lemon juice

Combine all the ingredients and serve as soon as possible. If not using at once, store in a container in the refrigerator for 1–2 days.

Serves 4 *(Pictured on front cover and page 114)*

tip *TO PEEL TOMATOES: Place them in a heatproof bowl and cover with boiling water. Allow to stand for 30–60 seconds, depending on the size of the tomatoes. Drain through a colander and peel.*

Red Curried Pork with Kumera & Lime

*The new cuts of pork are quick to cook and are very lean.
This is a creamy textured curry that has a refreshing lift of lime.
Serve with a bowl of freshly cooked jasmine rice.*

1 tablespoon canola oil

1 onion, chopped

1 tablespoon red curry paste

500 g lean diced pork or
cubed pork fillet

1 cup water

2 medium-sized kumera,
peeled and sliced

200 g cauliflower florets

3 kaffir lime leaves (optional)

1 red capsicum, cut into strips

200 g green beans, trimmed
and cut into 3 cm pieces

2 teaspoons fish sauce

2 teaspoons palm sugar or
brown sugar

juice of 1 lime

2 tablespoons plain skim-milk
yoghurt

a handful of basil leaves, torn
(see tip)

1. Heat the oil in a wok or frying pan and cook the onion until soft but not coloured. Add the curry paste and stir for 2–3 minutes over a medium heat. Add the pork and stir to coat with the curry mixture.

2. Stir in the water, then add the kumera, cauliflower and kaffir lime leaves. Cook until the vegetables are tender but not mushy, 10–15 minutes. Add the remaining ingredients and cook for 5–7 minutes.

3. Just before serving stir through the basil and yoghurt.

Serves 4

 Basil leaves will not darken if they are torn rather than chopped with a knife.

Adding fresh herbs just before serving provides a real flavour and fragrance boost to the dish.

This page: *Chilli Avocado Steaks* (page 112) with *Onion & Tomato Salsa* (page 112)
Opposite: *Citrus Pork Steaks* (page 116) with *Stir-fried Vegetables* (page 116)

Citrus Pork Steaks

finely grated zest of 1 orange

1 teaspoon five-spice powder

2 tablespoons canola oil

4 pork loin steak medallions

2 garlic cloves, chopped

1 teaspoon grated fresh ginger

3/4 cup orange juice

1/4 cup lemon juice

1 tablespoon sweet chilli sauce

1 teaspoon cornflour mixed
with 1 tablespoon water

sliced flesh and fine slivers of
zest of 1 orange (garnish)

1 quantity Stir-fried Vegetables
(this page)

1. Combine the orange zest, five-spice powder and 1 tablespoon of the oil. Spread the mixture onto both sides of meat and set aside for 15 minutes to allow the flavours to infuse.

2. Heat the remaining oil in a frying pan over a medium to high heat and cook the pork until lightly brown on both sides. Remove the pork, drain on a paper towel and set aside.

3. Add the garlic, ginger, orange and lemon juices, sweet chilli sauce and cornflour mixture to the pan and bring the sauce to the boil. Reduce the heat and add the pork to the pan. Cover and cook over a low heat, turning the pork once until it is creamy in colour, 2–3 minutes on each side.

4. Serve on a bed of Stir-fried Vegetables garnished with the orange slices and orange zest.

Serves 4 *(Pictured on page 115)*

Stir-Fried Vegetables

*Wonderful served as a base for meat, poultry, fish or tofu dishes.
Or simply serve with rice or noodles.*

1 tablespoon canola oil

1 red onion, sliced

250 g green beans, sliced

1 small red capsicum, seeds
removed, cut into strips

100 g snow peas, trimmed

2 teaspoons sweet chilli sauce

1. Heat the oil in a frying pan or wok and stir-fry the onions and green beans over a high heat for 2 minutes. Add the capsicum and stir-fry for 2 minutes.

2. Add the snow peas and cook until just tender, but still a vibrant green colour, 3–5 minutes. Stir through the sweet chilli sauce and serve.

Serves 4

Sweet Chilli Ginger Pork Kebabs

These are a colourful option to pop on the barbecue, or else cook them quickly under a hot grill. Serve with Quick Vegie Couscous (page 47), or slide the pork and vegetables off the skewers onto crisp leaves of cos lettuce or warmed souvlaki bread to make a delicious easy-to-eat 'wrap'.

2 tablespoons salt-reduced soy sauce

2 teaspoons grated ginger

1 teaspoon sweet chilli sauce

$1/2$ teaspoon sesame oil

450 g pork fillets, cut into 2 cm cubes

1 red and 1 green capsicum, cut in half, seeds removed

8 bamboo skewers, soaked in water for 30 minutes

1. Mix the soy sauce, ginger, chilli sauce and sesame oil together. Add the pork, cover and marinate for at least 1 hour in the refrigerator.

2. Cut the capsicums into triangles and thread them onto the skewers alternately with the pork.

3. Cook on a hot barbecue or under a hot grill, basting once with any remaining sauce.
(Take care not to overcook – pork cooks very quickly and needs to be juicy inside to taste best.)

Serves 4

 For a vegetarian alternative, replace the pork with 500 g firm tofu or tempeh.

This page: *Psychedelic Sauce* (page 129) with *Creamy Polenta* (page 136)
Opposite: *Spinach Frittata* (page 128)

eat! enjoy!

Fast FOODS at home

Get fast at home! You may be 'out of fresh' but now you won't be out of fresh ideas.
Here are some great ideas for whipping up a host of delicious impromptu
meals using goodies from the pantry and freezer. These dishes are so delicious
you will want to use them even when you have fresh ingredients to hand,
so we have provided tips for 'adding a touch of fresh' to many of the recipes.

Freezer & Pantry Checklist

Use the following checklist so you always have goodies on hand to create a range of exciting, tasty and nutritious dishes.

Stock up the Freezer with...

A variety of breads and rolls: wholemeal and multigrain, French breadstick, mountain bread, roti, bagels, English-style muffins, pita bread, focaccia, seedy bread such as soy and linseed, pumpernickel, rye, souvlaki bread and pizza bases and bake-at-home rolls.

Pasta and noodles such as gnocchi, tortellini, ravioli, lasagna and Hokkien noodles.

Frozen vegetables such as peas, sweet corn (cobs and kernels), broccoli, pumpkin pieces, chopped onions, cauliflower, spinach, beans, carrots, frozen chopped onions and vegetable mixes such as Chow Mein Mix, Whole Green Beans and Carrots and Mediterranean Vegetables.

Frozen fruits such as strawberries, raspberries, blackberries and mango pulp.

Frozen meat, fish and poultry such as lean beef, pork and lamb, seafood and skinless chicken pieces and fillets.

Stock up the Pantry with...

A variety of breads and rolls, including wholemeal and multigrain rolls, French breadstick, mountain bread, roti, bagels, English-style muffins, pita bread, focaccia, seedy bread such as soy and linseed, pumpernickel, rye, souvlaki bread, pizza bases, tortillas, fajitas and burritos.

Pasta such as penne, tagliatelle, shells, fettuccine, bow-tie (butterfly), fusilli, vermicelli, lasagna, spaghetti, tortellini, ravioli, tortelli, rigatoni, corn pasta.

Noodles such as Hokkien noodles, egg noodles, rice noodles, soba noodles and cellophane noodles.

Canned vegetables (preferably salt reduced or no added salt varieties), such as whole and crushed tomatoes, Tomatoes & Herbs, beetroot, artichoke hearts, corn kernels and creamed corn.

Prepared pasta sauces, salsas and tomato paste.

Fruit canned in its own juice or water.

Dried fruits such as apricots, pears, peaches, prunes, figs, raisins, sultanas, currants, apples, pawpaw and mango.

Dried, canned and vacuum-packed cooked beans, peas and lentils, such as red kidney beans, borlotti, lima, cannellini, soy, broad beans, green or brown lentils, split yellow lentils (channa dhal) and split red lentils, chick peas, split peas and baked beans.

Milk varieties, such as long life low-fat and reduced fat milk, reduced-fat calcium-enriched soy drink, canned evaporated low-fat milk and skim milk powder.

Nuts – raw or roasted and unsalted – such as peanuts, pistachio nuts, macadamia nuts, walnuts, pecan nuts, cashew nuts, hazel nuts, pine nuts and blanched, slivered and flaked almonds.

Canned seafood, such as tuna, salmon, shrimps, crabmeat and sardines.

Dried herbs, such as basil, oregano, parsley, sage, thyme, rosemary, dill, mint, tarragon, fennel, chives and bay leaves.

Dried spices, such as cinnamon, cloves, cardamom, allspice, ginger, mixed spice, nutmeg, turmeric, pepper, cayenne, paprika, dill seed, caraway seeds, chillies (dried whole, chilli flakes and ground chilli powder), cumin, coriander and vanilla beans.

Bottled prepared crushed or chopped fresh herbs and spices, such as garlic, ginger, chillies, coriander and lemongrass.

Condiments (preferably low-salt or salt-reduced) such as soy sauce, fish sauce, oyster sauce, sweet chilli sauce, chilli and garlic sauce, stock cubes, powders and long-life packs of prepared stock.

Vinegar, such as wine (white and red), cider and balsamic.

Monounsaturated and polyunsaturated vegetable oils such as olive oil and canola oil.

Chilli Bean Soup with Corn Chips (opposite)

Chilli Bean Soup with Corn Chips

Creamy, corny and spicy all at once, this rich soup is sure to please young and old alike. Adjust the amount of chilli sauce according to your palate.

1 tablespoon olive oil

1 onion, chopped

1 x 810 g can salt-reduced crushed tomatoes

1 x 420 g can red kidney beans, drained

1 x 420 g can creamed corn

1 cup frozen peas

1 teaspoon crushed garlic

1–2 teaspoons chilli sauce

2 cups water

cracked black pepper

100 g salt-reduced corn chips for serving

1. Heat the oil in a large saucepan and stir-fry the onions over a high heat for 1 minute. Reduce the heat, cover and cook over a low to medium heat for 5 minutes.

2. Stir in all the remaining ingredients except for the corn chips, then bring to the boil over a medium heat, stirring to prevent the soup from sticking to the bottom of the pan.

3. Serve piping hot in wide shallow bowls with the corn chips tucked around the outside.

Serves 4

FOR A FRESH touch...

Top with a generous spoonful of Carnival Capsicum Salsa (page 39) or Avocado & Coriander Salsa (page 38).

When using canned vegetables, especially if using several types in one dish, choose the salt-reduced variety when available. Otherwise the salt content can become quite high.

Quick & Slick Vegetable Chowder

With a one, two, three of the good old can opener,
you'll have this yummy soup – much better than
dialling out for a not so healthy take-away!

1 x 420 g corn kernels, drained

1 x 300 g can butter beans, drained

½ teaspoon crushed garlic

375 ml low-fat evaporated milk

1 cup vegetable stock

1 cup small shell pasta

200 g frozen broccoli florets

60 g parmesan, grated

cracked black pepper

1. Put all the ingredients except the cheese and pepper in a medium-sized saucepan and bring to the boil over a medium heat, stirring occasionally to prevent the soup from sticking to the bottom of the pan.

2. Reduce the heat and cook until the broccoli is tender, about 10 minutes. Stir in the cheese and the pepper and serve piping hot.

Serves 4

FOR A FRESH touch...

Serve topped with a generous spoonful of Zesty Herb Sprinkle (page 97) or Onion & Tomato Salsa (page 112).

Spinach Enchiladas

The savoury filling is made in minutes from convenient ready-prepared ingredients, and is ideal for a variety of 'wraps' such as tacos, enchiladas, pancakes, pita rounds and burritos.

1 tablespoon olive oil

1 onion, chopped

350–400 g lean minced topside beef or 1 cup couscous

2 tablespoons tomato paste

1 teaspoon crushed garlic

1/3–1 cup water

250 g frozen spinach, thawed

pepper or chilli powder

10 Enchilada Tortillas

1 x 425 g can Tomatoes & Herbs

1 cup shredded mozzarella or reduced-fat cheddar cheese

1. Heat the oil in heavy-based saucepan and stir-fry the onions over a high heat for 1 minute. If using beef, add it to the pan and continue to cook over a high heat, stirring constantly, until the meat changes colour. If using couscous, add it to the pan and stir over a high heat for 1 minute.

2. Stir in the tomato paste and garlic. If using beef, stir in 1/3 cup water, reduce the heat and simmer for 5 minutes. If using couscous, stir in 1 cup water, but do not simmer.

3. Add the spinach to the pan, stirring to heat it through. Season with the pepper.

4. Prepare the tortillas according to the directions on the packet, then fill each one with about 2 heaped tablespoons of the beef (or couscous) mixture. Roll the tortillas up and place them in a large ovenproof dish.

5. Top with the Tomatoes & Herbs, sprinkle with cheese and cook under a preheated hot grill. Alternatively, bake in a preheated oven at 200°C until the cheese bubbles and browns lightly, 8–10 minutes.

Serves 4-6

tip *If you are out of fresh onions, try using frozen chopped onions available at supermarkets. 1 cup frozen chopped onions is equivalent to 1 large onion.*

Tofu Cacciatore with Fettuccine (opposite)

Tofu Cacciatore with Fettuccine

In this dish, bite-sized pieces of tofu languish in a tasty Italian-inspired sauce that drizzles enticingly through the fettuccine. For a delightful texture contrast, serve with crostini or grissini sticks. You can replace the tofu with sliced lean skinless chicken fillets.

1 tablespoon olive oil

1 onion, chopped

1 x 425 g can salt-reduced crushed tomatoes

1 x 300 g can sliced champignons in brine

1 teaspoon crushed garlic

2 tablespoons tomato paste

1/4 cup white wine

500 g firm tofu, thickly sliced

2 tablespoons Pesto (page 36)

cracked black pepper

1. Heat the oil and stir-fry the onions over a high heat for 2 minutes. Reduce the heat and stir in the tomatoes, mushrooms, garlic, tomato paste and wine. Bring the sauce to the boil, then reduce the heat and cook over a low to medium heat for 20 minutes.

2. Bring a large pan of water to the boil and cook the fettuccine until *al dente*. As soon as it is cooked, drain the pasta and set aside.

3. Preheat the grill. Cut the tofu slices in half on the diagonal. Brush the tofu with the pesto, dust with the pepper, then cook under a hot grill for 2 minutes on each side. Set aside to cool and firm.

4. Add the tofu to the sauce and cook uncovered over a low to medium heat for 10 minutes. Arrange the fettuccine on serving plates and top with the tofu and sauce.

Serves 4

 **ON occasion!**

Serve with slices of garlic bread alongside.

Rosemary Stanton's
Spinach Frittata

Rosemary Stanton is one of Australia's best-known nutritionists. In 1998, she was awarded the Order of Australia medal for her services to community health through education in nutrition and dietetics. Rosemary appears regularly on Burke's Backyard and lectures to doctors, medical students, sporting teams and members of the public. She is the author of 25 books on health and nutrition, the latest being: *Good Fats, Bad Fats; Healthy Vegetarian Eating; Find out About Fibre and Vitamins.*

This is a tasty 15-minute dish. If you are feeding only two people, pop the leftovers in the refrigerator because this frittata is just as good served cold the next day. For a fresh touch, serve with a tossed green salad and cherry tomatoes.

1 tablespoon extra-virgin olive oil

1 onion, chopped

2 garlic cloves, crushed

1 teaspoon dried basil leaves

1 x 420 g packet frozen spinach

8 eggs, lightly beaten

pepper

40 g parmesan, shaved with a vegetable peeler

1. Heat the oil in a heavy-based frying pan and stir-fry the onions, garlic and basil over a low to medium heat for 2–3 minutes. Increase the heat to medium, then add the frozen spinach and cook until it defrosts, turning it several times.

2. Pour the eggs over the spinach and cook until the egg is set, lifting the edge of the frittata to allow any uncooked egg to run underneath.

3. Dust with the pepper, top with the cheese, cut into wedges and serve.

Serves 4 *(Pictured on page 119)*

tip *Try making mini frittatas for a change. Combine the cooked onion and spinach with the eggs. Spoon the mixture into a muffin tray that has been brushed with a little olive oil. Bake in a preheated oven at 190°C until the frittatas are cooked through and lightly browned.*

Psychedelic Sauce

If you are whipping up a meal from the pantry shelves, you may as well go all the way with colour! Spoon on top of Creamy Polenta (page 136) or fettucine. Or serve alongside patties or burgers, kebabs, filo rolls or roasted or barbecued meats.

1 tablespoon olive oil

1 teaspoon crushed garlic

1 small onion, chopped

1 cup frozen carrot rings or sticks

1 x 320 g can shredded beetroot, drained well

1 x 320 g can corn kernels, drained well

1 x 810 g can whole peeled tomatoes

1 teaspoon dried basil

1 teaspoon dried oregano

pepper

1. Heat the oil in a medium-sized saucepan and stir-fry the garlic, onions and carrots over a medium to high heat for 1 minute. Remove from the heat and stir in the beetroot, corn, tomatoes, basil and oregano.

2. Bring to the boil, then reduce the heat, cover and cook over a low to medium heat for 12–15 minutes, stirring occasionally to prevent the sauce from sticking to the bottom of the pan.

3. Season with the pepper and serve.

Serves 4 *(Pictured on Page 118)*

tip *Using canned shredded beetroot in this sauce adds a blast of colour and sweet and sour undertones.*

Duo Pesto Pasta (opposite)

Duo Pesto Pasta

This recipe is brought to life with two types of pesto — a great standby for impromptu meals. Serve hot as a main meal or cold as a tasty salad with a generous squeeze of lemon juice.
If you don't have any home-made pesto sauce tucked away in the freezer, use bottled sun-dried tomato pesto and sweet basil pesto, which are available at larger supermarkets and delicatessens.

500 g penne pasta

250 g frozen green peas, beans or broccoli

1/2 cup sliced semi-dried tomatoes

3 tablespoons Semi-dried Tomato Pesto (page 36)

3 tablespoons Sweet Basil Pesto (page 36)

cracked black pepper

1. Bring a large pan of water to the boil. Add the pasta and cook until *al dente*, 10–15 minutes.

2. Meanwhile, steam your choice of green beans, peas or broccoli until tender but still bright green.

3. Drain and divide the pasta into two lots. Return half to the cooking pan and the other to a large bowl.

4. Add the Semi-dried Tomato Pesto and the semi-dried tomatoes to one half. Add the Sweet Basil Pesto and your choice of green vegetables to the other. Toss each lot of pasta to evenly cover with pesto. Arrange side by side on serving plates and serve immediately.

Serves 4

FOR A FRESH touch ...

Serve scattered with whole or sliced fresh basil and accompany with a salad of leafy greens including spinach or rocket leaves.

Cottage Pasta Roll-Ups

These are so delicious you'd never believe they were so quick and easy to make. Serve with bread or rolls warmed in the oven for 10 minutes. (Bake-at-home rolls can be taken straight from the freezer and cooked in the same oven.)

1/4 teaspoon oil

200 g fresh lasagna sheets

2 x 200 g cartons onion-and-chive flavoured cottage cheese

200–250 g frozen spinach, thawed

1 cup low-fat evaporated milk

2 garlic cloves, crushed

1 x 425 g can Tomatoes & Herbs

1/2 cup shredded mozzarella

1. Preheat the oven to 180°C. Brush the inside of a large ovenproof dish with the oil.

2. Cut the lasagna sheets in half and spread with the cottage cheese, then dot with the spinach. Roll up the pasta firmly and, using a sharp knife, cut each roll in half. Place the rolls, seam side down, in the prepared dish.

3. Place the evaporated milk, garlic and Tomatoes & Herbs in a saucepan and bring to the boil over a medium heat. Reduce the heat, and simmer for 2 minutes.

4. Pour the sauce over the pasta rolls, sprinkle with cheese and bake in the preheated oven for 30 minutes.

Serves 4

ON OCCASION!

When you have spread the fresh lasagne with the cottage cheese, top with lean sliced ham before rolling up and baking.

Tomato & Orange Pasta with Tuna

A quick-and-easy pan-tossed dish. For a fresh touch,
stir in ½ cup chopped Italian flat-leaf parsley and serve
with a mixed green salad.

300 g linguine, vermicelli, spaghetti, penne, farfalle or spiral pasta

1 x 185 g can tuna in oil

1 tablespoon olive oil

1 onion, chopped

½ teaspoon crushed garlic

1 x 425 g can crushed tomatoes

½ cup orange juice

8–12 pitted olives, cut in half

1 tablespoon finely grated orange zest

cracked black pepper

1. Bring a large pan of water to the boil and cook your choice of pasta until *al dente*. As soon as it is cooked, drain the pasta and set aside.

2. Drain the tuna over a large frying pan to catch the juices. Add the olive oil and heat the pan. Add the onion and cook, stirring, over a medium to high heat until softened, 4–5 minutes. Add the garlic and cook for 1 more minute.

4. Add the tomatoes and orange juice and simmer the mixture for 3 minutes. Stir through the tuna, olives and orange zest, and cook for 1 more minute.

5. Season with the pepper and immediately toss through the cooked pasta, or serve separately with sauce spooned on top.

Serves 4

tips *Always have some finely grated orange zest tucked away in the freezer for adding a zesty touch to sauces like this as well as to desserts and cakes.*

Replace the black olives with 3 tablespoons toasted pine nuts or 2 tablespoons capers or 4 anchovy fillets rinsed in water and chopped.

Pepper Crusted Rack of Lamb (opposite) with *Plum & Cranberry Sauce* (opposite) and *Quick Vegie Couscous* (page 47)

Pepper Crusted Rack of Lamb

People would never think that this impressive dish could be whipped up from pantry and freezer ingredients! Serve with roasted pumpkin (available frozen) and steamed frozen green peas and you will have a feast. Or to add a Middle Eastern flavour, serve with Quick Vegie Couscous (page 47) which can be prepared using frozen vegetables.

1/4 teaspoon oil

a rack of lamb with 8 cutlets, well trimmed

2 tablespoons cracked black pepper

1 quantity Plum & Cranberry Sauce (this page)

1. Preheat the oven to 200°C. Brush a small baking tray with the oil.

2. Brush the lamb with a little of the Plum & Cranberry Sauce. Sprinkle the pepper on a sheet of greaseproof paper and roll the lamb evenly in the pepper.

3. Bake in the preheated oven for 20–30 minutes or until the lamb is just pink inside. Allow the meat to rest for 10 minutes in a warm place before slicing.

Serves 4

Plum & Cranberry Sauce

A great sauce for adding a tangy fruity flavour to a variety of dishes such as patties, kebabs, and roasted or barbecued meat and poultry.

1/2 cup bottled cranberry sauce

1 x 825 g can plums, drained, stones removed, chopped

1 tablespoon balsamic vinegar

1. Combine all the ingredients in a saucepan and bring to the boil slowly, stirring.

2. Simmer until the mixture thickens, 5–10 minutes. If not serving at once, store in a covered container in the refrigerator for up to 1 week.

CReaMy Polenta

Polenta is traditionally prepared with lashings of butter or cheese,
but it can be very successfully prepared with low-fat milk with just
a touch of parmesan. Serve it with Psychedelic Sauce (page 129)
or with other saucy dishes such as Vegie Pasta Sauce (page 45)
or Honest to Goodness Beef Stew (page 110).

3 teaspoons olive oil

1 small onion, chopped

1 cup vegetable stock

**3 cups low-fat milk or
calcium-enriched soy drink**

1 cup fine polenta (cornmeal)

**3 tablespoons grated
parmesan**

cracked black pepper

1. Heat the oil and stir-fry the onion over a high heat for 1 minute. Remove from the stove and add the stock and milk. Bring the mixture to the boil and gradually add the polenta, stirring constantly.

2. Cook, stirring, until the polenta is thick and creamy, and no longer grainy, 10–15 minutes. Remove from the heat and stir in the cheese and pepper.

3. Serve at once, or spread out evenly in a loaf tin or flan tin that has been brushed with a little oil. Set it aside to cool and harden, then cut it into desired shapes and cook under a hot grill until lightly browned.

Serves 4 *(Pictured on page 118)*

Tuna with tomatoes & chick peas

This is one of Rosemary Stanton's favourite quick recipes — it takes only 15 minutes to prepare. As a bonus, it is high in fibre and nutrients and low in fat. Serve in bowls accompanied by crusty bread. (Bake-at-home rolls from the freezer are ideal, and only take 5 minutes to cook.)

12 dried tomatoes

3/4 cup boiling water

1 tablespoon extra-virgin olive oil

1 onion, chopped

1/2 teaspoon crushed garlic

1–2 teaspoons chopped chillies

1 x 425 g can tomatoes

1 x 420 g can chick peas, drained

1 cup frozen peas

1 x 400 g can tuna in spring water, drained

2 teaspoons dried salad herbs

1. Place the dried tomatoes in a heatproof bowl. Pour the boiling water over and cover with a plate or lid and set aside.

2. Heat the oil in a large saucepan and stir-fry the onion, garlic and chilli over a low to medium heat for 3–4 minutes. Add the tomatoes, chick peas and frozen peas. Bring the mixture to the boil, then reduce the heat and simmer for about 3 minutes.

3. Add the tuna, salad herbs and the dried tomatoes in their soaking water. Cook over medium heat for 2 minutes, stirring gently to combine the ingredients without breaking up the tuna too much. Serve at once.

Serves 4

FOR A FRESH touch...

Sprinkle with lots of chopped parsley.

Jambalaya (opposite)

Jambalaya

This hasty-tasty one-pot Cajun dish is based on the New Orleans version of a Spanish paella and is a meal in itself.

1 cup quick-cooking brown rice

1 x 250 g packet frozen Broccoli, Yellow Bean and Capsicum Mix

1 tablespoon canola oil

1 onion, chopped

1 teaspoon Cajun spice mix

1 x 425 g can Tomatoes & Herbs

1 x 300 g can red kidney beans, drained

1. Cook the rice according to the directions on the packet. Drain and set aside.

2. Meanwhile, steam the frozen vegetables or cook them in a microwave oven until tender. Set aside.

3. Heat the oil in a large saucepan, add the onions and spice mix and stir-fry over a high heat for 2 minutes.

4. Add the steamed vegetables, tomatoes and beans and bring the mixture to the boil. Reduce the heat slightly and cook until the liquid reduces and thickens, 3–4 minutes.

5. Stir in the rice and cook over a low heat until heated through, about 5 minutes.

Serves 4

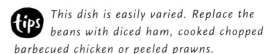 *This dish is easily varied. Replace the beans with diced ham, cooked chopped barbecued chicken or peeled prawns.*

For a fresh touch, whip up a crisp salad while the dish is bubbling on top of the stove. A mixture of cos lettuce, endive, watercress and sliced spring onions drizzled with a Lime Dressing (page 99) complements this dish well.

Asian-Style Stir-Fried Beef

It's easy to complete this meal — simply cook some rice while the beef is marinating.

2 teaspoons cornflour

1 tablespoon mirin or dry sherry

1 teaspoon sesame oil

2 tablespoons salt-reduced soy sauce

400 g rump steak, trimmed of fat and thinly sliced

1 tablespoon peanut oil

1 onion, chopped

1/2 teaspoon crushed garlic

1 teaspoon chopped ginger

200 g frozen broccoli

1 cup frozen green beans

1/4 cup water

1. Using a wooden spoon, combine the cornflour, mirin, sesame oil and soy sauce in a bowl. Add the meat and stir to ensure that all of the slices of meat are evenly coated. Allow the meat to absorb the flavours for at least 15 minutes.

2. Heat the oil in a wok or frying pan and cook the onion, garlic and ginger until soft but not browned. Toss in the meat and cook over a high heat for 2–3 minutes.

3. Add the broccoli, beans and water to the pan and cook until the vegetables are just tender but retain their vibrant green colour.

Serves 4

FOR A FRESH touch...

Enjoy experimenting with some of the Asian greens that are now becoming widely available. If the greens have fleshy stalks you can use them in stir-fries. Try replacing the broccoli and beans with 1/2 bunch each bok choy and Chinese broccoli (or other Asian greens).

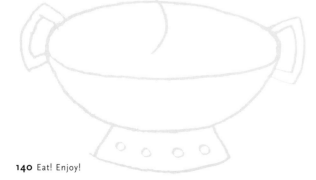

Korma Chow Mein

A simple noodle idea that combines stir-fried beef or soy-beans with Chinese vegetables and seasonings. For a fresh touch top with sliced spring onions, including the green tops, and serve with lemon wedges.

1 x 375 g packet fresh Hokkien noodles

2 tablespoons canola oil

400 g thinly sliced beef strips or 1 x 425 g can soy beans, drained

1–2 tablespoons mild curry paste such as korma

1 x 500 g packet frozen Chow Mein Vegetable Mix

2 tablespoons lemon juice

2 tablespoons unsalted roasted peanuts (garnish)

1. Cook the noodles according to the directions on the packet. Drain and toss with 1 teaspoon of the oil.

2. Heat the remaining oil in a wok or large frying pan over a high heat, add the beef (or soy beans) and curry paste and stir-fry over high heat for 1 minute. If using beef, transfer it to a plate and set aside.

3. Add the frozen vegetables to the pan. Reduce the heat to medium, cover and cook for 3–4 minutes. Remove the lid and add the noodles, lemon juice and beef. Heat through. Use two forks to fluff up the noodles

4. Arrange on serving plates, sprinkle with the peanuts and serve.

Serves 4

tips *Before freezing meat, slice or chop it first, then freeze in the amount you will need for one meal – much easier than trying to hack your way through a large frozen lump!*

You can buy prepared lemon juice in bottles. Store in the refrigerator once opened.

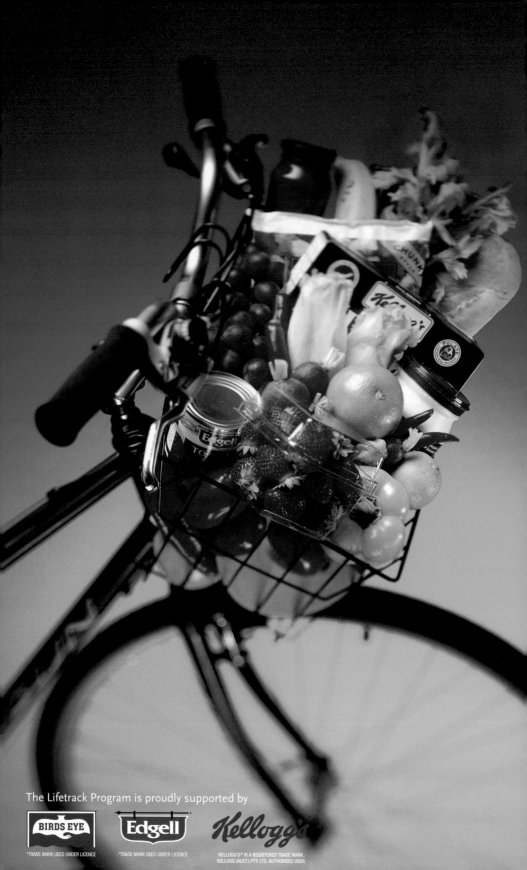

The Lifetrack Program is proudly supported by

get your life on track with Lifetrack

There is now overwhelming evidence that what we eat plays a vital role in determining our health and well being. In this chapter, we explain how the innovative Lifetrack program can help us make changes to our daily eating habits which could reap health rewards and reduce our risk of cancer and heart disease.

Assessment-based Program

To take part in the Lifetrack program participants fill in a questionnaire about their eating habits and lifestyle. The questionnaire is then analysed and a comprehensive individualised report is produced. The report, which identifies any areas where the diet needs to be modified, is sent to the participants with a copy of the *Lifetrack Dietary Guide*. This book includes user-friendly information about eating for health and recipes from celebrity food-lovers. Participants in the Lifetrack program use the report and the information in the dietary guide to make positive changes to their diet. To order an assessment, simply phone 13 3310. The cost of participating in the program is $35.

Lifetrack Clears Away Confusion

Dr Graham Giles, Lifetrack's senior researcher, explains, 'The last decade has seen a mass of diet-related information circulating in the media. People pick up a little information about what they should eat, and the next week they hear that they should stop eating something they thought was healthy. So many people are very confused and that's one of the reasons we developed the Lifetrack program. We have used current research to formulate the program and provide people with accurate information.'

Lifetrack manager Paul Davey advises, 'It is never too late to make changes to daily eating habits which could reap health rewards and reduce your risk of cancer and heart disease. Even the smallest changes can make a difference. Lifetrack helps you find that starting point, and helps end the confusion about fad diets. It allows people to regain control of their eating habits.'

Research Findings

The first results of the Lifetrack assessments, based on a sample of 5000 participants, confirmed that Australians are eating too much fat, not enough foods rich in calcium and iron, and not enough vegetables and fruits that contain essential nutrients and vitamins. The findings also revealed that most Australians have little knowledge of their own food intake and nutritional requirements.

Dr Giles urges Australians to take stock of their eating habits, saying, 'Up to 30 to 40 per cent of cancers are related to diet and may be prevented by changing the type, and amount, of food we eat.' Lifetrack applauds the typical Mediterranean diet, which is based on vegetables, fruit, pasta and bread, with only a little meat. This way of eating is recognised as the key to reducing the risk of cancer and other serious diseases.

Eat! Enjoy! has been designed in direct response to Lifetrack's research findings. Each chapter focuses on particular foods that have been identified as requiring special attention, and the recipes in each chapter provide practical ways to include more of the particular foods in everyday eating.

Here we briefly explain the nutritional profile of the foods in each of the chapters and provide a list of even more recipes based on these foods, which are scattered throughout the book. We have also included tips for low-fat, high-flavour dishes and healthy snacks, including a reference to specific recipes in this book which demonstrate the ideas.

But before we explore further the specific nutrition issues identified by the Lifetrack program, let's meet two of the many people who have participated in the program, celebrities Lyn Talbot and Athol Guy.

Lyn Talbot

Lyn Talbot is a director of *Ella Media,* a company specialising in freelance journalism, corporate video production and media relations. As a television personality and writer, Lyn's hectic lifestyle often makes planning meals difficult. However, since the end of the Ten Network's popular *Healthy, Wealthy & Wise* program, Lyn has been able to establish more of a routine with her diet and to some degree, plan her shopping and meals.

Lyn watches her diet no matter which far flung and exotic country she might be visiting. So she was a little surprised to discover in her recent Lifetrack assessment that her carbohydrate intake was down and she needed to increase consumption of foods such as pasta, bread and rice.

Lyn says, 'When I was working on *Healthy, Wealthy & Wise* the travel was often intense. On the road the crew had no choice but to eat out for breakfast, lunch and dinner. It was always bliss to arrive home and be able to cook what I felt like. I still travel regularly, but I am in a much better position to look after myself and I now watch that I take in enough carbohydrates and have a wide variety of foods. I follow the advice provided in my Lifetrack report and eat pasta twice a week, rice once a week and grain breads every day.'

Lyn enjoys seafood and eats fish regularly. During the day she snacks mainly on fruit, but also enjoys rice crackers and dips, banana smoothies and nuts, especially almonds. Lyn often pushes herself too hard, becomes tired and her weight drops. She said exercise and good food help maintain her weight.

'I am conscious of what I eat, but I don't miss out on things I love, I simply eat them every now and again within a very balanced diet. One of my great indulgences is my regular Sunday slap-up of bacon, eggs and tomatoes. I just love it and I won't go without it, but it is a once-a-week-only treat,' Lyn explains.

'I know the Lifetrack program stresses the benefits of physical activity and fortunately I have always enjoyed exercise. I try to include five sessions of exercise a week and that might mean a run, walk, golf, or a game of tennis.' Once a week Lyn runs around the Caulfield racetrack as the horses are training early in the morning. It is one of the weekly rituals that she has grown to love, come rain or shine.

'I have travelled to over 35 countries and I have never seen such a diversity of food anywhere else. The availability of an extraordinary range of foods from many cultures and cuisines makes cooking at home, or dining out in Australia, an absolute pleasure. Just thinking about it is making me feel hungry,' Lyn says.

Athol Guy

Athol Guy became one of Australia's most recognisable musicians when he and three others formed *The Seekers* in 1963. The band split in 1968 and reformed again in 1993. *The Seekers* are still together and intend to release a compilation album in 2000, as well as touring Australia, the UK and New Zealand. When not travelling around the world playing his double bass, Athol is kept busy with his Melbourne-based business consultancy.

Athol calls himself a food larrikin. He enjoys cooking, loves to eat and is willing to try a variety of foods. Until recently he thought his diet was excellent, but participating in the Lifetrack program has encouraged him to think twice about what he eats. According to Athol's personalised assessment he needs to eat more fruit and vegetables. Since taking part in the Lifetrack program, Athol has discovered a whole new range of vegetables and now enjoys including them in his planned meals, usually dinner.

'I went to a Malaysian restaurant a few months ago and tasted okra and sugar peas for the first time. Now I eat a lot of them, as well as bok choy, which is fabulous. For some reason I had also forgotten how great fresh peas taste, so they are back on the menu at home,' Athol says.

He now tries to eat five servings of vegetables a day instead of three, which was his daily intake before Lifetrack. Athol makes sure he has plenty of fruit at home, which makes it easy to eat the two servings of fruit recommended by the program. He particularly enjoys fresh stone fruits and putting other fruits through a juice machine.

'Lunchtime is not a well-planned meal for me. I don't eat just because it is that time of the day - I wait until I am hungry then grab a sandwich, or go to one of the food halls around Melbourne where every type of fruit and vegetable is available in a variety of ways,' Athol explains. 'Another great way of getting the right amount of vegetables and a variety of colours and tastes is to use the pre-prepared packs available from supermarkets and fruit and vegetable shops. It means you can throw together a stir-fry if you get home late because you don't have to worry about the preparation.'

'I am also really conscious of the connection Lifetrack makes between physical activity and health. I know I have improved my diet in a lot of ways, but I still have to improve my exercise. In summer, I swim every day – sometimes three times a day – and I aim to swim at least once a day in the colder months. However, I need to keep up with my walking because, although I swim, I am not one for getting into the pool and doing a set number of laps each time. The other reason I need to walk each day is for my dog's sake. Both of us need to hit the track again,' Athol says.

Breads & cereals

Breads and cereals are rich in carbohydrates, fibre, protein, iron and B-group vitamins. They are also low in fat and kilojoules so there is no need to avoid them if you are watching your weight. A diet high in breads and cereals may help to lower the risk of heart disease, obesity, diabetes, certain cancers and some bowel disorders. A minimum of five serves, but preferably more, is recommended each day for good health.

One serve of breads and cereals is equivalent to: 1 slice of bread or 1/2 cup breakfast cereal or 3/4 cup cooked pasta and rice.

High-carbohydrate, high-performance foods include: pasta, all types of rice, all types of bread, crisp breads and water crackers, breakfast cereals, noodles, couscous, polenta, scones, muffins, cakes and loaves.

Recipes based on these foods can be found in Chapter 1 (pages 10–25). Apart from the specially designed recipes in Chapter 1, try these other recipes:

- Risotto with Mediterranean Vegetables & Bok Choy (page 33)
- Zucchini Spice Muffins (page 48)
- Choc o' Beet Muffins (page 49)
- Gabriel Gaté's Pear & Prune Loaf (page 64)
- Light & Luscious Apple Crumble (page 65)
- Gnocchi with Pumpkin & Broccoli (page 75)
- Mozzarella Pesto Pizzarets (page 81)
- Middle Eastern Spiced Lamb Roll-ups (page 105)
- Chilli Bean Soup with Corn Chips (page 123)
- Spinach Enchiladas (page 125)
- Duo Pesto Pasta (page 131)
- Cottage Pasta Roll-ups (page 132)
- Creamy Polenta (page 136)
- Jambalaya (page 139)

Vegetables & Legumes

Vegetables and legumes are rich in nutrients such as vitamin C, beta-carotene, folate, dietary fibre and potassium and are low in fat and kilojoules. Additionally, legumes are good sources of protein and iron. Vegetables and legumes also contain a range of substances called phytochemicals which further assist in preventing diseases such as heart disease and cancers. Currently, Australians are not eating enough vegetables and legumes. *Eat! Enjoy!* is full of exciting and tasty ways to help you eat the recommended amount of five serves of vegetables and legumes each day.

One serve of vegetables and legumes is equivalent to: 1 small potato or 2 tablespoons cooked vegetables or 3/4 cup salad vegetables or 1/2 cup cooked legumes.

When you think 'vegetables' remember all these types: fresh vegetables, frozen vegetables, canned vegetables (preferably salt-reduced), dried legumes, canned cooked legumes, vacuum-packed cooked legumes and marinated vegetables.

You'll find a host of appetising, quick and easy ways to enjoy all these types of vegetables in Chapter 2 (pages 26–49). Vegetables star in popular dishes like dips and spreads, sauces, pasta, pizza, casseroles, filo parcels, soups, foods for the barbie, and even muffins.

Apart from the specially designed recipes in Chapter 2, try these recipes:

- Mushroom Spinach Couscous with Chick Peas (page 17)
- Spinach & Pumpkin Lasagna (page 20)
- Stir-fried Rice with Vegetables & Cashews (page 21)
- Rice Volcanoes (page 24)
- Vegetable Pasta with Balsamic & Basil (page 23)
- Vegie Wraps (page 25)
- Creamy Asparagus Soup (page 73)
- Gnocchi with Pumpkin & Broccoli (page 75)
- Kumera, Corn & Pasta Soup (page 76)
- Golden Vegetable Rolls with Ricotta (page 77)
- Tofu Vegetable Skewers (page 79)

- Bocconcini & Roasted Tomato Salad (page 83)
- Thai Beef Salad (page 107)
- Honest to Goodness Beef Stew (page 110)
- Mushroom Minute Steaks (page 111)
- Chilli Avocado Steaks (page 112)
- Stir-fried Vegetables (page 116)
- Chilli Bean Soup with Corn Chips (page 123)
- Quick & Slick Vegetable Chowder (page 124)
- Spinach Enchiladas (page 125)
- Psychedelic Sauce (page 129)
- Jambalaya (page 139)
- Korma Chow Mein (page 141)

Fruits

Fruits are rich sources of carbohydrates, dietary fibre, beta-carotene and vitamin C and they are also low in fat and kilojoules. Like vegetables and legumes, fruits contain a range of phytochemicals. Eating sufficient fruits (and vegetables and legumes) can help reduce blood pressure and blood cholesterol and can help people with diabetes control their blood sugar levels. It may also help to prevent obesity, heart disease and certain cancers. We should aim to eat at least two serves of fruit each day.

One serve of fruit is equivalent to: one average-sized piece of fruit or 1/2–1 cup fruit canned in water or juice.

A range of delicious fruit recipes is featured in Chapter 3. So now you can enjoy more fruit on different occasions throughout the day. Remember all these types of fruits: fresh fruit, fruit canned in its own juice, frozen fruit, fruit purees and dried fruits.

Apart from using the specially designed recipes in Chapter 3 (pages 50–69), try these other delicious fruity recipes:

- Karen Inge's Bircher Muesli (page 12)
- Fruity Porridge (page 13)
- Banana Spice Muffins (page 16)
- Purple Blaze (page 45)
- Great Grape Lassi (page 89)
- Amazing Apricot Lassi (page 89)
- Creamy Coulis (page 91)
- Mini Mango Freezecakes (page 91)
- Citrus Pork Steaks (page 116)
- Plum & Cranberry Sauce (page 135)

Dairy & Soy

You'll find enticing ways of increasing your calcium intake in Chapter 4 because dairy foods such as milk, yoghurt and cheese are the best sources of calcium which can be readily absorbed by the body. Low-fat and reduced-fat dairy products are a particularly good source of calcium – great news, seeing that we are urged to go for low-fat products to help reduce our fat intake.

For those who omit dairy foods from their diet, such as vegans, calcium-enriched soy drink is a good source of calcium. So is tofu (bean curd) that is prepared using calcium sulphate. However, many other foods also contain good amounts of calcium, such as: canned fish with the bones, whole wheat bread, cauliflower and broccoli, bok choy, Brussels sprouts, rocket and watercress, kale, parsley, almonds, sesame seeds and sea vegetables such as nori (see glossary).

Go for calcium daily. It's important to consume calcium-rich foods daily. The body has a limited ability to absorb calcium and therefore needs to take in small amounts frequently. For people who don't enjoy drinking milk, other milk products can be incorporated in the diet in convenient and tasty ways. For example, skim-milk powder can be added to cakes, scones, muffins, milk drinks and desserts. Evaporated low-fat milk adds a surprising creaminess to soups, pasta sauces and desserts.

Apart from the specially designed recipes in Chapter 4 (pages 70–93), try these other delicious calcium-rich recipes:

- Geoff Jansz's Italian Autumn Salad (page 34)
- Orange & Tandoori Yoghurt Dip (page 53)
- Cantaloupe with Orange Sherbet (page 61)
- Cherry Yoghurt Freezes (page 63)
- Cherry Yoghurt Thick Shakes (page 63)
- Apricot Yoghurt Cream (page 67)
- Spinach Enchiladas (page 125)
- Cottage Pasta Roll-ups (page 132)
- Creamy Polenta (page 136)

Meat, Fish & Chicken

You'll find easy ways to increase your iron intake in Chapter 5 because these foods are particularly high in the type of iron that is readily absorbed by our bodies. This type of iron is called haem iron. Animal foods also contain another type of iron called non-haem iron. This is the type of iron that plant foods contain, and, unfortunately, it is not as readily absorbed by our bodies. Non-haem iron is more readily absorbed when eaten with other foods such as: foods containing haem iron, such as meat, poultry or fish; foods rich in vitamin C such as capsicums, citrus fruits and parsley.

Enjoy eating a host of iron-rich foods, to ensure the total iron intake is adequate (viva variety!) — lean beef; lamb and pork; lean skinless chicken pieces and fillets; a range of seafood; eggs; dried, canned and vacuum-packed cooked legumes; wholegrains including a range of breakfast cereals, especially enriched cereals.

Apart from using the specially designed recipes in Chapter 5 (pages 94–117), try these other delicious iron-rich recipes:

- Mushroom Spinach Couscous with Chick Peas (page 17)
- Chicken, Tabouli & Nori Wraps (page 19)
- Lentil Soup with Roasted Capsicums (page 28)
- Chilli Pumpkin Soup with Chick Peas (page 29)
- Sesame Tuna Steaks with Salsa (page 39)
- Vegetable Chicken Kebabs (page 40)
- Yellow Lentil Mash (page 40)
- Ricotta & Chicken Balls with Apricot & Coriander (page 80)
- Pesto Lamb with Mediterranean Vegetables (page 103)
- Chilli Bean Soup with Corn Chips (page 123)
- Rosemary Stanton's Spinach Frittata (page 128)
- Tomato & Orange Pasta with Tuna (page 133)
- Pepper Crusted Rack of Lamb (page 135)
- Asian-style Stir-fried Beef (page 140)
- Korma Chow Mein (page 141)

Fast Foods at Home

Getting fast at home is often more economical than rushing out or dialling out for fast foods. The bonus is that it allows you to keep track of the fat, salt and added sugar you are consuming. Eating take-away or fast foods occasionally is not a problem but as our lifestyles become progressively busier, many of us turn too often to fast foods for help. It's true that they solve the immediate problem of feeding hungry tummies quickly, but quick fixes are often not the ideal solution. This is certainly the case when it comes to many of the fast take-away foods available today.

As Rosemary Stanton, one of Australia's top nutritionists, explains, 'Most people have days when they have little time to prepare a meal. There is always the temptation to turn to fast foods, but most are a nutritional disaster and don't taste nearly as good as a home-cooked meal. If you have a few tricks up your sleeve, you can get a meal ready in less time than it takes to whip out for a take-away. As a bonus, home cooking will have more flavour and nutrients, and much less saturated fat.'

Chapter 6 includes many dishes that can be quickly prepared using foods from the pantry and freezer. It also features a Freezer & Pantry Checklist to use as a guide for stocking up the pantry and the freezer with plenty of nutrient-packed foods.

Apart from using the specially designed recipes in Chapter 6 (pages 118–141), enjoy modifying other recipes in this book, using ingredients from the pantry and freezer. Here are some examples to get you started:

- Stir-fried Rice with Vegetables & Cashews (page 21): Use a 500 g packet frozen Chow Mein Vegetable Mix instead of the fresh vegetables.
- Vegie Pasta Sauce (page 45): Use 1 cup frozen chopped onions and a 250 g packet frozen Mediterranean Vegetables instead of the Fresh vegetables.
- Quick Greens (page 47): Use a 250 g packet frozen broccoli, 2 cups frozen green beans and 1 cup frozen peas instead of the fresh vegetables.
- Apple Berry Strudel (page 60): Use thawed frozen berries instead of the fresh berries.

Hints For Healthier Take-Aways

When you are caught 'on the hop with no time to shop' there are some 'healthier' take-away options to go for:

- pizzas prepared with lots of vegetables and/or lean beef or seafood (go easy with the cheese, and keep fatty toppings such as pepperoni and salami to a minimum, or eat them only occasionally)
- lean skinless chicken in a bun with plenty of salad
- lean burgers in a bun with plenty of salad
- foccacia with lots of vegetables
- baked jacket potatoes – hold the butter and margarine and ask for just a dollop of sour cream, or replace it with a heaped spoonful of cottage cheese. Top with one or two salads and just a little cheese.
- chunky chips – although they are 'fatty' they are much less fatty than French fries, other thin chips and small potato products such as potato gems.
- rotisserie chicken with the skin removed, wrapped in souvlaki bread with salad

- grilled fish – the batter on fish acts like a sponge and soaks up lots of cooking fat or oil. (If you don't believe it, next time you treat yourself to good old fish and chips, pop a piece of fried battered fish or a potato cake on top of a napkin or brown paper bag, fold it over the food and press it gently. The napkin or brown paper will become translucent after coming in contact with fat!)
- felafel or lean lamb in souvlaki bread with lots of salad and a squirt of chilli sauce

Fast From the Supermarket

Make some time to peruse the variety of 'fresh-prepared' meal items from larger supermarkets. You may be surprised at the amount and quality of the fresh-prepared foods you can purchase for the same price as fast take-away foods. Try:

- fresh-prepared beef, chicken or vegetarian lasagne. Team up with packs of washed salad greens and fresh tomatoes and bake-at-home rolls
- fresh pasta with prepared pasta sauce sprinkled with chopped fresh vegetables such as capsicums and spring onions
- canned fish with a packet of fresh salad greens and a prepared potato salad
- fresh noodles cooked quickly and tossed with stir-fried pre-sliced vegetables or frozen vegetables and seasoned with sweet chilli sauce

Tips For Healthy Snacks

Having a range of healthy snacks on hand is a great opportunity to increase variety in our diets, and helps cut down on the amount of fatty, salty, sugary snacks that are readily available and, unfortunately, all too convenient! Try a variety of fresh and dried fruits, fruits canned in their own juice, plain and fruit yoghurt, uniced fruit buns, plain and toasted sandwiches, scones, crispy fresh vegetable sticks such as carrots, capsicums and celery and crisp breads with thin slices of cheese.

There are plenty of delicious snack recipes scattered throughout this book, such as:

- Breakfast Pancakes (page 15)
- Banana Spice Muffins (page 16)
- Chicken, Tabouli & Nori Wraps (page 19)
- Vegie Wraps (page 25)
- Zucchini Spice Muffins (page 48)
- Choc o' Beet Muffins (page 49)
- Mango & Macadamia Whirl (page 69)
- Berry Banana Smoothie (page 69)

- Tasty Tofu Dip (page 72)
- Amazing Apricot Lassi (page 89)
- Great Grape Lassi (page 89)
- Vanilla Iced Coffee on the Rocks (page 92)

Leftover cooked dishes such as:
- Rice Volcanoes (page 24)
- Kumera & Cashew Patties (page 42)
- Rosemary Stanton's Spinach Frittata (page 128)

Tips For Low-Fat, High-Flavour Dishes

All the recipes in this book have been developed to keep the fat content low without compromising on the taste and texture of the dishes. Here are some tips for achieving low-salt, high-flavour dishes with examples of specific recipes that use these methods:

Go for herbs and spices:
- Chilli Jam (page 25)
- Chilli Pumpkin Soup with Chick Peas (page 29)
- Sweet Basil Pesto (page 36)
- Macadamia Chilli Ginger Pesto (page 37)
- Avocado & Coriander Salsa (page 38)
- Pineapple Mint Salsa (page 55)
- Mango Chilli Jam (page 55)
- Yoghurt & Chilli Sauce (page 80)
- Duré-Dara's Grilled Chicken with Wasabi & Herbs (page 104)
- Gentle Coriander Beef Curry (page 109)

Go for citrus rind, juices or vinegar:
- Vegetable Pasta with Balsamic & Basil (page 23)
- Avocado & Coriander Salsa (page 38)
- Corn Salsa (page 38)
- Carnival Capsicum Salsa (page 39)
- Citrus Salsa (page 59)
- Zesty Herb Sprinkle (page 97)
- Lime Dressed Salad (page 99)

Go for marinades:
- Tofu & Vegetable Skewers (page 79)
- Dill & Ginger Marinated Fillets (page 98)
- Chicken & Lemongrass on Parade (page 100)
- Sweet Chilli Ginger Pork Kebabs (page 117)

Go for long slow cooking:
- Ian Parmenter's Lamb Shank & Tomato Ragout (page 106)
- Honest to Goodness Beef Stew (page 110)

Go for stir-fries:
- Stir-fried Rice with Vegetables & Cashews (page 21)
- Quick Greens (page 47)
- Asian-style Stir-fried Beef (page 140)

Go for roasting:
- Lentil Soup with Roasted Capsicums (page 28)
- Roasted Red Capsicum Sauce (page 35)
- Garlic Roasted Vegetables (page 43)
- Roasted Pumpkin & Beetroot Salad (page 44)
- Roasted Garlic Potato Mash (page 102)

Glossary

Balsamic Vinegar
A sweet and spicy vinegar with a full-bodied flavour. Available from supermarkets and delicatessens.

Besan Flour
Also known as chick pea flour. Used for binding patties, burgers and batters. Available from supermarkets and Indian grocery stores.

Breadcrumbs
To make fresh breadcrumbs, carefully drop pieces of day-old bread down the chute of a food processor while it is operating and process until the desired consistency. Use at once, or freeze until required.

Cardamom Pods
Impart a sweet appealing flavour to both savoury and sweet dishes. Available from supermarkets and Asian grocery stores.

Cinnamon Stick
Used to flavour sweet and savoury dishes and is usually removed before serving. Available from supermarkets, delicatessens and Asian grocery stores.

Coconut Milk
Use 'light' coconut milk to keep the fat content low. Available canned and dried from supermarkets, Asian grocery stores and delicatessens.

Coriander
Both fresh coriander leaves and ground coriander seeds impart a distinctive pleasant flavour to savoury dishes. Available from supermarkets, delicatessens and Asian grocery stores.

Couscous
Popular in Middle Eastern dishes, couscous is tiny pellets made from semolina (the inner part of wheat) and water, coated with flour. Available from delicatessens and supermarkets.

Cumin
Imparts a caraway flavour to savoury dishes. Available from supermarkets, delicatessens and Asian grocery stores.

Fennel Seeds
Impart a licorice-like flavour to savoury dishes. Available from supermarkets, delicatessens and Asian grocery stores.

Fish Sauce
A strongly flavoured sauce made from salted fish and used in Asian cooking. Available from Asian grocery stores and supermarkets.

Five-spice Powder
A mixture of cinnamon, cloves, star anise, fennel and black pepper. Available from supermarkets and delicatessens.

Garam Masala
An Indian blend of spices. Available from Asian grocery stores.

Garlic
Chopped garlic has a milder flavour than crushed garlic. To roast garlic, place whole unpeeled heads of garlic on a baking tray. Bake at 180°C for 20–25 minutes, and when cool, remove the skins. Leave the cloves whole for antipasto platters, or mash and add to vegetable mashes, soups or sauces.

Hokkien Noodles
Golden-coloured fresh noodles available from supermarkets and Asian grocery stores.

Horseradish
The root of a plant with a hot pungent flavour. Horseradish sauce is available in jars from delicatessens and supermarkets.

Kaffir Lime Leaves
Dark green glossy leaves from a variety of lime tree. Tear or shred and add to soups, marinades and curries to impart an aromatic citrus flavour. Available fresh or frozen from Asian grocery stores.

Lemongrass
Popular in South-East Asian cooking. Imparts a distinctive citrus flavour. Available from Asian grocery stores.

Mirin
A Japanese sweet cooking wine. Available from supermarkets, Asian grocery stores and health food stores. Dry sherry can be used instead.

Mountain Bread
Otherwise known as Lavash bread. A Middle Eastern bread which comes in thin rectangular sheets. Available from supermarkets and delicatessens.

Nori
Made from sea vegetables pressed into thin sheets and dried. Available from Asian grocery stores, health food stores and supermarkets.

Palm Sugar
A richly flavoured sugar with a fudge-like texture. Used in South-East Asian cooking. Available from Asian grocery stores. Dark brown sugar can be used instead.

Polenta
Also known as cornmeal. A golden-coloured meal especially popular in Northern Italian cooking. Available from supermarkets and delicatessens.

Ricotta Cheese
A soft, fresh, mild-flavoured cheese. Packaged baked ricotta has a firm texture and can be sliced and used in many dishes. Available from supermarkets and delicatessens.

Saffron
The dried stamens of the crocus flower. Used to flavour and colour a variety of dishes. Available from delicatessens and Asian grocery stores.

Tabasco Sauce
A fiery hot sauce available from supermarkets and delicatessens. Use sparingly.

Tandoori Paste
A spicy paste used to colour and flavour foods before cooking. Available from Indian grocery stores.

Tempeh
A 'cake' of partially cooked fermented soy beans, held together by a dense white mould similar to the 'crust' on Camembert and Brie. Marinate and roast or grill until golden brown. Available from health food stores.

Teriyaki Sauce
A rich dark sauce used in Asian cooking. Available from supermarkets and Asian grocery stores.

Tofu
Made from soy beans and also known as bean curd. Commonly used in Japanese and Chinese cooking. Available from supermarkets, Asian grocery stores and health food stores.

Turmeric

A brilliant golden yellow spice with a peppery flavour. Available from supermarkets and Asian grocery stores.

Wasabi

Japanese horseradish. Available as a powder or as a paste from Asian grocery stores and supermarkets. Use sparingly.

Zest

Thin aromatic outer layer of the skins of citrus fruits which is usually removed by grating. A vegetable peeler can also be used to remove strips of zest which can then be cut into thin slivers with a small sharp knife. (First wash citrus fruits thoroughly in soapy water to remove dust and wax).

Cook's Notes

Fresh herbs are used unless otherwise stated. When ginger is called for, use fresh root ginger unless other types are specified. Use freshly ground black pepper unless cracked black pepper is noted. Use plain skim-milk yoghurt. Use salt-reduced soy sauce. Use calcium-enriched soy drink. 60 g eggs have been used to test the recipes containing eggs. Use mild-flavoured honey and mild-flavoured oils unless specific types are called for. Use raw nuts or dry-roasted nuts to keep fat to a minimum (regular roasted nuts are usually deep-fried).

Use a blender or a food processor to 'blend' food. The microwave cooking times have been calculated according to the use of an 850 watt microwave oven. If your microwave oven is a lower wattage you may need to increase the specified cooking times; if it is a higher wattage, you may need to reduce the specified cooking times.

Remember to use only microwave-proof dishes and microwave-safe plastic wraps.

Weights & Measures

For accurate measurements, you will need:

- a graduated set of four cups measuring 1 cup, 1/2 cup, 1/3 cup and 1/4 cup for ingredients such as flour, sugar or chopped vegetables. Level cup measures are used.

- a litre measuring jug (4 cups) or a 250 ml measuring cup for measuring liquids.

- a graduated set of 4 spoons measuring 1 tablespoon, 1 teaspoon, 1/2 teaspoon and 1/4 teaspoon. Level spoon measures are used.

INDEX